With A Little Help From His Friends

To Les and Elsie
Our recently made
and now treasured
friends. You also
have a son to be proud of.
love, Gloria and Jim

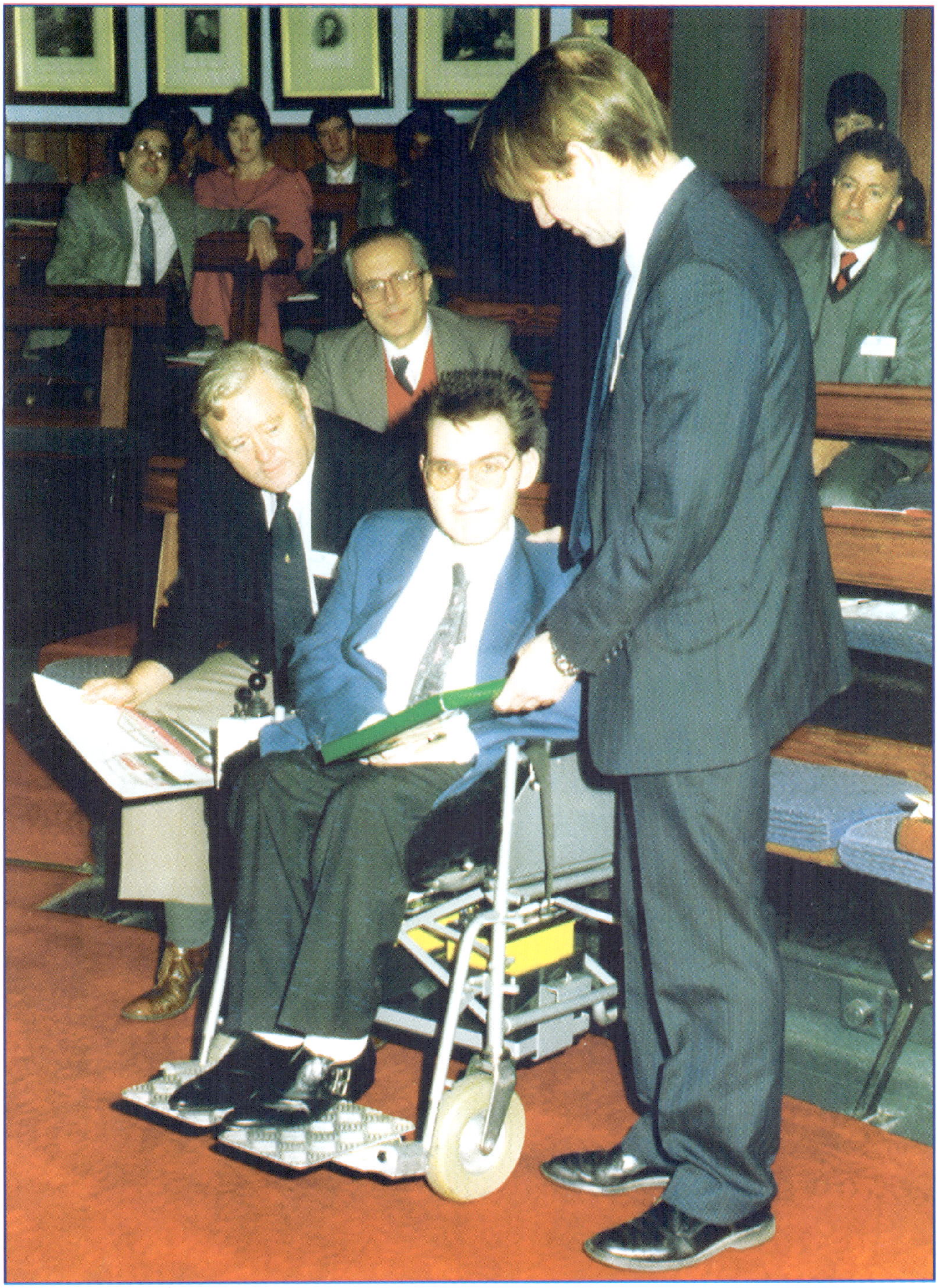

Michael at the International Muscular Dystrophy Colloquium
held in the Liverpool Medical Institution on 22nd October 1987.
He is being presented with a gift by Professor Richard Edwards in admiration
and recognition of his achievements in spite of severe disability.

Photographs by kind permission of Professor Richard Edwards

Published Tuesday 23rd March, 1999 by
Gloria Thomas (The Michael Thomas Book Fund)

ISBN 0 9535349 0 1

Printed in Wales by L Pugh & Son Colour Printing

CONTENTS

Acknowledgements

General support of the project to publish this book has been amazing and there have been many very generous donations towards the printing costs. I cannot name everyone but I would like to thank them all most sincerely.

My husband, Jim, who has been a tower of strength throughout.

My mother-in-law Fan and my Mum and Dad, who are always so supportive and who also generously donated towards the printing costs.

Professor Richard Edwards, Mr Gwyn Jones, Mr Tony Lee of the Muscular Dystrophy Group and Kate Fox of The Neuromuscular Centre for their advice and encouragement.

My dear friend, Margaret Jones, for starting the fund off with a generous donation in memory of her husband Cyril. She has also given tremendous help in the fund-raising generally.

My employers, Carter Jonas, Chartered Surveyors, for their generous donation and kind interest in the project.

My niece Lisa and her friends Phillippa, Vicky and Rosie the dog for their sponsored walk!
Plus everyone who sponsored them!
Everyone who helped to make the Table Top Sale such a success.

Graham and Pat Lewis for organising a very successful Social Evening at Llanymynech Golf Club.

The Social Committee and many friends at Llanymynech Golf Club for the proceeds of a Raffle.

Everyone who donated prizes for various Raffles for my cause.
The Country Garden Plant Centre, Hadnall, Shrewsbury.
Mrs Jennifer Pugh in memory of Mrs Annie Pugh.

Mrs Barbara Ellis
Mr and Mrs Den Oakley
Mrs Audrey Evans
Alison & Kevin Swanton
Mike and Trina Lewis

Mrs Lucy Owens
Mr and Mrs Alec Atherton
Mr John and Mrs Muriel Jones
Marion and Bill Williams
Mr and Mrs R Braid

and many many more.

Foreword

Michael Thomas made a deep impression on me as a person with indomitably good humour and courage in the face of adversity. His was also the best example of the way in which willing participation in research can help not only the individual but others similarly afflicted. Clinical research depends on mutual respect, trust and co-operation between the patient and the clinical scientist. Our knowledge of the benefits of weight control in Duchenne muscular dystrophy is almost entirely due to Michael's dogged determination to get rid of excess weight. His reward was the regaining of the ability to propel himself in a hand operated wheelchair after years of being dependant on an electric wheelchair for his mobility. For me there was the privilege of studying Michael's metabolism to confirm that weight control could be done safely without accelerating muscle wasting. We learned something of the complex effects of muscular dystrophy on muscle metabolism, and this emphasis on weight control became a practical step forward in patient care. Similarly the work on sleep and breathing led to practical ways of helping muscular dystrophy sufferers with breathing difficulties though it did not, to our disappointment, prove to help Michael. Over all the period of surgery and repeated hospital visits, Michael remained in good humour, always seeking to make the best of the situation and pressing on with his remarkable talent in art and design which he went on to study at College.

In the field of research on muscle diseases much has been learned over the past quarter of a century yet there is still no cure for the muscular dystrophies. We hear of prevention, and we hope earnestly for cure but let us not forget that those like Michael, impaired by muscular dystrophy, disabled by weak muscles compounded by weight gain and deformity, are in reality enabled or handicapped by the society in which they live.

Michael had the advantage of the love and devotion of parents who cared for him wonderfully with the support of the staff and facilities of the nearby Robert Jones and Agnes Hunt Orthopaedic Hospital, Oswestry. All who knew Michael would agree, I believe, that while we mourn his early death yet we are sure that the world is a better place for his having spent time in it.

Gloria's moving account is an untouched record of her memories and feelings of those years when she and Jim lived with and for Michael and his muscular dystrophy. "With a little help from his friends" is a fitting tribute to Michael and an important reminder that while muscular dystrophy still cannot be cured there is treatment and beyond that, healing, which I hope will be the greater for Gloria and Jim as Michael's saga is made available as a source of inspiration to others.

Richard Edwards

Introduction

As each of us pass through this world we make friends along the way. Friends at home, friends at work and friends in the community. Some become lifelong friends, having earned our affection, respect and trust, helping us along no matter how hard the journey, cheering us up when we are down and not forsaking us when they fail. They stick by us through thick and thin, whatever our circumstances, never letting us down. These are the friends who make our lives worthwhile.

My son Michael, severely disabled with Duchenne Muscular Dystrophy, made many friends all through his short life and with a little help from his friends he experienced a quality of life which would have been impossible without them.

This book is an account of Michael's life - the good and the bad. It's a tribute to him and a dedication to all his friends, in particular four special friends who brought a lot of sunshine and joy into the latter half of his life.

Chapter I
The Early Years

Jim and I were both brought up in the village of Porthywaen, four miles from the Shropshire market town of Oswestry. As teenagers we met at Porthywaen Youth Club, which was held in the function room of the local Red Lion Inn at Porthywaen every Thursday evening. We fell in love and were married on 29 February 1964. Living initially with Jim's parents, we eventually got a house in Oswestry. We were convinced that our first child was going to be a boy and we had planned to name him Andrew Graham Thomas, but sadly he was stillborn. We eventually got over it, I became pregnant again and gave birth on 25 May 1966 to a beautiful, blue-eyed, dark-haired baby boy. We named him Michael Andrew Thomas and he was the light of our life. His grandparents and two great grandmothers doted on him.

Michael thrived and as he got older his hair turned blonde. He was a delightful toddler, lovable and mischievous, developing like any other child.

We moved back to Porthywaen when Michael was 18 months old, to the same house that I had been brought up in by my grandmother. She herself had moved to Penybontfawr, nearer to her old home at Llangynog. 'Nain' (Welsh for grandmother), as we called her, was very attached to Michael and we tried to visit her as often as we could.

Our old neighbours at Oswestry, Edna and Sandra Gray had been very fond of Michael too. They kept in touch and visited us from time to time. They always called him 'Twinkle'.

Jim's parents saw Michael every day now that we lived in the same village but, unfortunately, our move to Porthywaen meant that my mother and stepfather didn't see so much of him. They missed him dreadfully. Occasionally they would call and take us out in the car. They often talk about these outings and recall everything Michael said and did.

Just before Michael was due to start school Jim's mother gave up her job and offered to look after him for me to go out to work. Money was a bit tight so I gratefully accepted her offer and got a job as a secretary in the local orthopaedic hospital, the world famous Robert Jones and Agnes Hunt Orthopaedic Hospital at Gobowen, Oswestry. Michael was quite happy being looked after by his grandma and when he started school she took him there every morning and collected him in the afternoon. If I couldn't get time off to go to school sports, etc. she went in my place. She always prepared our evening meal, too, which was a great help to me. Michael naturally became very attached to his gran, who he called 'Fan' because everyone else did. Although I enjoyed my work I sometimes felt I missed out on a lot of precious moments with Michael and there were times when I was quite jealous of Fan.

When Michael was about four years old we got him a dog. She was a brindle coloured Staffordshire Bull Terrier called Candy and she had a lovely personality. Michael and Candy were great friends. We trusted her totally with Michael and we had her until he was about eight years old. Jim made her a nice kennel in a sheltered spot at the back of the house. Candy was a very loud snorer and you could hear her from inside the house.

Soon after I started work Fan took Candy over to live with her because it wasn't fair to leave a dog alone all day. Michael never tired of hearing about the mischief she would get up to whilst he was out at school all day. One day when the refuse collectors called, she took a dislike to one of them when he threw the plastic bin lid at her and chased him into next door's garden. He managed to get away but Fan had to go round and get her by the scruff of the neck because she didn't have a collar on. After that, whenever it was dustbin-emptying day Fan had to offer Candy biscuits to make her come into the house before the dustcart came round.

Another funny thing Candy did was when my brother-in-law Bob, who liked to play practical jokes, brought a toad into the house in a bucket to show to his mum and I because he knew we would scream and Michael would laugh.

"Get it out of here!" Fan screamed and as Bob went to the back door and gently threw it out into the garden, Candy dived with open mouth and gulped the toad down. It happened so quickly that we couldn't believe it. It was like something out of a Tom and Jerry cartoon. Michael was doubled up with laughter and so were we.

We were a bit concerned about Candy swallowing a whole live toad but she suffered no ill effects.

In 1971 Michael began to fall over rather a lot. He had a peculiar way of running and also an odd way of climbing stairs but we thought this was just his funny little way of doing things. Then Fan attended Michael's first school Sports Day that summer and reported back to us that his clumsiness and awkwardness of movement compared with the other children worried her and she suggested we should get him checked over by the family doctor. When Dr Hughes examined Michael he said that he was very flat-footed and this could be causing his walking and running difficulties, so he referred him to Mr Gordon Rose, a Consultant Orthopaedic Surgeon at the hospital where I worked. Having worked in his clinics, I knew Mr Rose personally and was pleased. While we awaited his appointment at the hospital, Michael fell at school and hurt his leg. We took him to the Casualty Department where the Registrar on duty could find nothing except for a strained calf muscle and flat feet. Several months later this same Registrar spoke to me and enquired after Michael. He was shocked to learn that he had failed to diagnose the main problem.

Mr Rose eventually saw Michael. He mentioned his flat feet but made a very long and detailed examination of his whole body, asking lots of questions. He told Jim and I that he would like to run some routine blood tests. He would then see Michael again when the results were to hand.

Two or three weeks went by. In the meantime I tried to find Michael's case notes but was unsuccessful. Although I knew it was unethical, I asked Mr Rose's secretary if I could read what Mr Rose had said. She said sorry, but she couldn't allow me to do that and, in any case, Mr Rose had gone to America for a few weeks and had asked his colleague, Mr Cowie, to explain the blood test results to me should they arrive before his return. Mr Cowie in fact had Michael's case notes and I would just have to be patient.

Chapter II
The Bombshell

Life went on as usual. I loved my work at the hospital and it took my mind off my worries a bit. Having become very interested in orthopaedic and medical matters, I often read patients' case notes. Updating some records one day, I began to read the notes of a five year old child seen at one of the Hospital's clinics. They read something like this:

'This little boy has been falling down more and more of late. On examination, he has thickening of both calf muscles. He walks with a flat-footed, slightly waddling gait, which is more pronounced when he runs. The child gets up from the floor exhibiting classical Gower's sign, climbing up his legs with his hands until standing. I fear he has Duchenne Muscular Dystrophy and will organise a muscle biopsy. To have a blood test today. Parents will not be told until diagnosis confirmed.'

The words seemed to stand out as I read them over and over. A chill ran through me. I had read something once about Muscular Dystrophy. It put people into wheelchairs. I got this 'gut feeling' that the purpose of Mr Rose's detailed examination of Michael was to rule out or confirm this disease. Michael's symptoms were almost identical to this child's.

I kept my fears to myself and one day soon afterwards Mr Cowie's secretary told me that he wished to speak to me. I felt quite shaky when I went along to see him. He told me that one of the blood test results was abnormal and this meant that Michael could have some type of muscle disease or something called polymyositis. Mr Rose was due back soon, would see Michael again in clinic and would explain in more detail to us.

When we saw Mr Rose again I felt sick as he told us that he would arrange for Michael to see the Neurologist, Dr Heron, who would probably arrange for a muscle biopsy to be done at North Staffordshire Royal Infirmary. Mr Rose spoke to me privately later and told me of his fears about Duchenne Muscular Dystrophy and his sincere hope that his diagnosis was wrong.

My grandmother wasn't very well at this particular time. We didn't want to worry her so we didn't tell her anything. She was later admitted to hospital with cancer of the pancreas and died. I'm glad she never knew about Michael's condition. She had suffered all her life with 'nerves' and the family always tried to keep any bad news from her.

In the meantime Michael had other medical problems in the form of recurrent tonsillitis. He was rather a thin child then and we always had trouble getting him to eat because of septic tonsils. During the waiting time to see Dr Heron, in October 1972 Michael had his tonsils removed at Maelor General Hospital in Wrexham. It was strange to see, on the second day after the operation, Michael actually running around the hospital dayroom as if there was nothing wrong with him. We never saw him run like that ever again.

He seemed very healthy after his tonsillectomy, started to eat well and put on weight. We wondered if perhaps Mr Rose was being over-cautious and we were worrying unduly, although Michael did continue to have falls.

Dr Heron was a very kindly and caring man and when he saw Michael he explained to us, in as gentle a manner as possible, that if muscle biopsy confirmed his and Mr Rose's diagnosis, there was no actual treatment for the disease and certainly no cure. It felt like ages waiting for this biopsy to be done and even longer awaiting the result.

Michael was eventually admitted to the Neurology Ward at North Staffordshire Royal Infirmary to have his muscle biopsy. It is very difficult to explain something like this to a five year old but we told him that the doctor was going to try to stop his legs aching and try and make them stronger.

My mother was very supportive at this time and she came with me to Stoke on Trent to stay for a few nights while Michael was in hospital there. That was a very emotional time.

The day the biopsy was being done Mum and I went shopping to try and take our mind off things. We were in a shop just looking at clothes and mum said, "I wonder if he's out of theatre yet?"

I said "Oh mum, what if the biopsy is positive? What are we going to do?"
Putting an arm round me she said, "I don't know, love. Try to take it one step at a time".
I then broke down in the middle of the shop and mum couldn't help it, she was crying too.

We hurried back to the hospital so that we would be there when Michael came round from the anaesthetic. He was very distressed, poor little fellow. He must have been in a lot of pain because the incision scar on the front of his thigh was quite extensive and they must have taken a large sample of muscle. It took a long time for us to succeed in calming him down. A traumatic day all round.

The diagnosis of Duchenne Muscular Dystrophy was confirmed in January 1973. We were told that the progress of the disease would affect Michael's large muscles, which would gradually weaken, he would need a wheelchair by the age of ten or eleven and would be prone to chest infections because of weakening chest muscles. Most boys with this disease did not live beyond the age of twenty years. We were devastated but decided to shut our minds off to the cruel diagnosis and help Michael get the most out of life. The whole family put up a sort of mental block to it. The most important thing was to keep Michael generally fit and as happy as possible.

My friends and colleagues at the hospital were very helpful and supportive throughout this emotional trauma.

Michael, aged 6 with his dog Candy

Michael, aged 8, on the beach at Tywyn.

Chapter III
'Jack's Ranch'

After the bombshell hit us we decided that the family should have a holiday that summer. Jim then worked for an aggregates firm, Rogers Readymix. One of his colleagues had a static caravan on the 'Neptune' site at Tywyn near Aberdovey, so we hired it and went to stay for a week by the sea. Jim's parents Fan and Mick came with us and we really enjoyed ourselves, especially Michael, the result being that we decided to buy our own static caravan. We looked over the ones for sale on the site and finally chose a 'Pemberton Rancher'. Arrangements were made for it to be fixed on site number 199 and on our first stay in it we named it 'Jack's Ranch' ('Jack' being Fan's pet name for Michael).

We were very proud of our new caravan which was a big, nine-berther. Although it was bigger than we would normally need, we had allowed for alterations and plenty of space for a wheelchair when the time came.

Some wonderfully happy times were spent at Jack's Ranch. Every Thursday night I would pack a weekend bag and on Friday we would depart for Tywyn as soon as Jim and I got home from work. When we got there we would have fish and chips before unpacking. Saturday would be spent relaxing and playing on the beach with Michael. He loved this weekend ritual and couldn't wait to get to Tywyn. We have this lovely photograph of Michael when he was about eight years old, standing on the wet beach in his shorts in the sunshine. We try not to notice the nasty scar on his right leg from the muscle biopsy.

We usually travelled to Tywyn with Fan and Mick in their car. One Friday night on the road, halfway to Tywyn, Fan said to Mick,

"Where did you put the caravan keys?"

He said, "You've got them haven't you?"

She said, "I haven't got them. You always have them and they're not where you usually put them on the dashboard".

There followed some frantic pocket searching and it was concluded that the keys had been left at home.

Suddenly a little head poked through the gap between the front seats, turned to Mick and a very cross little voice exclaimed "you forgetless nit"! We all laughed so much it didn't matter that we had to travel back about 30 miles for the keys. To this day, if anyone in the family forgets something we say "You forgetless nit!"

One Sunday while at the caravan we decided to go to a place called 'Happy Valley' by car and then walk to the 'Bearded Lake' which we had heard a lot about from fellow caravanners. Apparently it is so called because of a weed that grows over it. Jim's Uncle Phil, Auntie Audrey and cousin Alison were visiting us this particular day and they accompanied us. It was a very warm day and although we were a bit dubious about Michael managing the walk, which was all uphill, we all agreed to take it in turns to carry him if he got tired. I'm afraid we had to carry him most of the way and it distressed us to see how the attempt had tired him. This was the first time we had witnessed the real difficulty Michael was experiencing with his walking and of course it got gradually worse. His grandma, having to get him to and from school, etc., knew only too well what his difficulties were and had warned us.

We hadn't seen any other children with Muscular Dystrophy before and in the early days during our times at the caravan, before Michael became completely wheelchair-bound, we met two brothers, Ian and Paul Dorricott, who were very severely disabled with it. We were shocked to see the deformities they had in their feet and spine but I knew, from working at the hospital, that it might be possible to minimise such deformities with physiotherapy and splints. At least I was in a position to get advice from physiotherapists at the hospital.

Michael was never told anything about his disability unless he asked. When he asked about the scar on his leg we just told him that he had a 'poorly leg' and had to have an operation to mend it. Later on, as he became more aware of his limitations of movement, we had to tell him that his muscles were not quite as strong as other boys' were so they got tired sooner. He didn't really question why this was so and just seemed to accept it. He did ask a very awkward question once, though, after he had seen the Dorricott boys.

He asked "Have I got the same thing wrong with me as Ian and Paul?"

We lied and told him that he had a different and milder variety of the disease. It may have been wrong of us, but after that we avoided passing the Dorricott family's caravan.

Chapter IV
Porthywaen School

We lived in the Parish of Llanyblodwel, which includes the villages of Llynclys, Porthywaen, Nantmawr and Llanyblodwel itself. Porthywaen School served all of Llanyblodwel Parish so it was the school that Michael attended. It was an excellent little primary school and, after moving out of the infants class to the junior class, Michael began to show good drawing skills. The school's many outings were followed by paintings and drawings of where they had been and what they had done, while at home he would have a pencil, crayon or felt-tip pen in his hand most of the time, drawing anything from insects to spaceships in fine detail. Later he developed a huge interest in all modes of transport - cars, lorries, trains, boats, aircraft and spacecraft. He also liked to write science-fiction stories.

From the time Michael was diagnosed with Muscular Dystrophy the school was kept informed and the Head Teacher Mr Mervyn Jones and his colleagues kept a weather eye open to protect Michael in the playground without making too much of his disability. As he gradually worsened, Mr Jones would report to us on the difficulties he experienced and the frequency of his falls. Gradually, at home, Michael could no longer get up the stairs so we needed to have a lift put in the house. The cogwheels of Social Services turn exceedingly slowly so my Uncle Reg generously paid for the installation of a lift, which ran from the kitchen into Michael's bedroom directly above. All we had to do was wind a handle to get Michael up or down. At school there were no stairs, just a few occasional steps that he needed help in climbing.

In the summer of 1976 Mr Jones suggested that a Care Assistant should be employed to meet Michael's special needs during school time. Fan already took him to school and collected him from there each day and would have been prepared to stay on at the school all day to attend to his needs but, to cover the Education Authority, it was necessary for there to be a formal employee doing this job and so it was somehow engineered for the Department of Education to employ her for this purpose. How lucky we were to have such consideration and co-operation. I dread to think how we would have fared today in the current financial and political climate.

Fan could tell a few tales about the time when she was Michael's Care Attendant at Porthywaen School. She took a great interest in all that happened at the school and in all the children there whom she knew. She was very protective of Michael and if any child did something a bit thoughtless or spiteful to him she was on them like a ton of bricks. Most of the children were very good with Michael.

The time came when a wheelchair was occasionally needed to get Michael around. I borrowed one from the hospital while we awaited delivery of Michael's own. This was ordered through the usual channels but took rather a long time to arrive. Goodness knows what we would have done if I hadn't been working at the hospital. After many complaints to the Department of Health in Birmingham the chair was eventually delivered. When it arrived there were plenty of volunteer helpers among Michael's school friends. They almost fought each other for a chance to push him around the playground. Fan had to give short shift to a few over-zealous wheelchair pushers!

There was one boy called Nigel who was hyperactive and had learning difficulties. He took a shine to Michael and loved to be allowed to push him around in his wheelchair. However, he would sometimes get a bit over-excited and when Fan took over, which she often had to do for Michael's protection, he would get quite upset. Nigel thought Michael was wonderful and hardly ever left his side. By the autumn of 1976 Michael was completely wheelchair bound.

Because of the fascination of the wheelchair, plus his sense of humour, Michael had no shortage of friends. His best friend was a boy called Brian Edwards. He was a farmer's son and I remember he always had trouble with his ears so he often wore a woolly hat pulled over them, even in summer if it was a windy day. I think some of the children teased him about this but Michael was very sympathetic so he tended to stick with him. Brian would often come to our house to play on a Saturday or Michael would visit his home. They were great pals. They would play the usual boyish games with toy cars and lorries, etc. We also had a large Leggo electric train set which they loved to play with. As it was difficult for Michael to play outside, he and Brian played mostly in Michael's room, which we had made larger by knocking two bedrooms into one to accommodate the wheelchair. Jim's brother Bob had a carpenter friend who had fitted one end of the room with a playtop, drawers and shelves for the trainset. Brian and Michael spent many a happy hour in there. Often they would just paint and draw. Brian had great admiration for Michael's drawings and paintings of cars, aeroplanes and spaceships.

"Do one for me, Mike" he'd say, so that he could take it home to show the family.

Our house was about a quarter of a mile from Porthywaen School and now that Fan had to push Michael to and from there in the wheelchair it was evident that this would not be very pleasant in bad weather. We therefore applied to the Education Department for transport to get him to and from school. This request was granted and a very nice gentleman called Mr James was employed to transport Michael and Fan to and from school every day. Mr James was very good with Michael and would have a laugh and a joke with him. Fan enjoyed talking to people and Mr James was no exception. They had a good natter every day.

That same year Mr Jones left Porthywaen School, being promoted to a bigger school. Everyone was sorry to see him go and we were no exception. We were a bit apprehensive as to what the new Head Teacher's attitude would be to a disabled pupil but we need not have worried, Mr Johnson was wonderful.

Michael, now permanently in his wheelchair when out and about, became a familiar sight in the village. Those who knew him would shout "Hello Michael" some would stop and chat, others would cross over the road embarrassed to look because they knew they couldn't hide their pity. This is something that most disabled people have experienced and felt angry about. Worse than that is when people do stop and talk but only to the parent or attendant as if the person in the wheelchair doesn't exist or has no brain or voice to converse.

We found it infuriating when, from time to time, some well meaning, usually elderly person would comment to us, in front of Michael, "What a terrible burden it must be for you".

"Certainly not" we'd retort indignantly. How dare they say such a thing about our son. In their ignorance, or their inability to comprehend how Michael or we could possibly be happy in such circumstances, what gave them the right to voice their pity? Perhaps I was too harsh on them;

after all, in their day Michael would have been put in a 'home'.

As Michael grew older and they got used to seeing him in his wheelchair people began to realise that although he couldn't walk he was happy and evidently his brain did work !

"They say he's very clever at drawing and knows an awful lot about aeroplanes", they'd whisper to each other as he went by.

I like to think that Michael helped to teach these people something and make them look at the disabled in a new light. This was probably true following an event that took place in July 1977.

Mr Johnson the Headmaster thought it would be a nice idea to mark the occasion of the Queen's Silver Jubilee by putting on a concert, for the senior citizens of Porthywaen and Llynclys, performed by the children. Michael volunteered to do a comedy act. We were delighted that his wheelchair didn't inhibit him from appearing on stage. He wrote himself a script. He didn't need any encouragement. When he had finished and we were allowed to read it, we were surprised to find how good it was.

On Children's Television at that time there was a programme that featured a Muppet type character called 'Doris'. Michael's idea was to incorporate a 'Doris' into his act as a ventriloquist's dummy. His 'Doris' was a stuffed green 'snake' draught excluder!

My mother and I attended the concert. I think Jim and Fan were visiting Mick who was in hospital at the time. The children all performed excellently although they were a little nervous.

When it came to Michael's turn he wheeled himself onto the stage where, smiling and rosy-cheeked at the friendly applause, clutching his script and trying very hard not to chuckle prematurely at his own jokes, he spoke to his audience:

"What do you think of the show so far?"
Mock choruses of "Rubbish!" echoed in reply.

They immediately warmed to him and when he had finished there was thunderous applause and there wasn't a dry eye in the house, including ours. That was a proud moment for me. The concert was the topic of conversation in the village for a long time afterwards and, though I say it myself, Michael had been the star of the show.

Before Michael could leave Porthywaen School we had to think about his secondary education. At the hospital where I worked they had a special school and I made enquiries about the possibility of his receiving secondary education there. We had to go through several official channels and eventually the Community Medical Officer attached to the Education Department, Dr Batcheldor, authorised and fixed this up with the Education Authority and the Health Authority. Dr Batcheldor was very kind and sympathetic to Michael and his problems and we were most grateful for his help and relieved that the next stage of Michael's education was taken care of.

Chapter V
Flying High

From the age of about nine years Michael became more and more interested in aeroplanes and he drew wonderful pictures of them in quite a lot of technical detail for his age. We bought weekly and monthly aeroplane magazines for him and he spent hours studying them. At home and at school he was encouraged to develop his drawing skills. Jim and I and Michael's grandparents also bought him lots of model aeroplanes to make. This stopped him from becoming bored when he couldn't go out to play and kept him occupied in the caravan at Tywyn if it rained.

Rita Jones, my friend and colleague at the hospital, fixed up a wonderful treat for Michael when he was 10 years old. The Oswestry Lions Club used to have a 'Grant a Wish' project every year, where some very deserving person was nominated by friends or relatives to be the recipient of a 'Jim'll Fix It' type of surprise. Rita felt that Michael was very deserving and she nominated him to the Lions for a special surprise. She wrote to them asking if they could arrange for Michael to see inside a helicopter or light aircraft. She knew a local family who had a small airfield near Chirk, which was only a few miles away, and she gave the Lions all the details. The Lions agreed to contact the Pierce family and so the surprise was fixed.

We found it very hard to keep the secret. The great day dawned and we told Michael we were taking him for an outing. He was rather taken aback when we only went as far as a farm in Chirk; we usually took him to the seaside at least! Eventually other people began to arrive in cars and Michael still looked a bit puzzled and disappointed but began to smile when he saw a small red Cessna plane coming in to land in one of the fields. Then a small group of people walked towards us, faces beaming. Mr Bill Strange of the Oswestry Lions came over and introduced himself to Michael and explained how Rita, who by this time had joined us, had nominated him for the Lions 'Grant a Wish' scheme. She had asked if Michael could see the inside of a helicopter or light aircraft but they had done better than that. He was to go up in the Cessna for a flight with pilot Captain Graham McConnell, who at that point joined them and introduced himself! By this time Michael was grinning from ear to ear.

Captain McConnell explained that he had to check the plane over but after that they would soon be off. In the meantime lots of people milled around, the local press took photographs, Rita was filming it all with her cine camera and then Michael was being lifted into the aircraft. He was quite the little celebrity and he loved it.

Before long they were off, up and away. They were away about an hour and when they landed everybody clamoured round to see Michael's reaction. I don't think he stopped smiling or talking for a week after that. The plane had dual controls and during the flight Captain McConnell had allowed him to take over the controls for a time. Before we left the airfield he presented Michael with a logbook recording the flight and showing a signed entry to say that he'd had 30 minutes of flying experience. That logbook has a special place amongst Michael's belongings.

It was Fan's idea that Michael's next birthday present should be a repeat flight with Captain McConnell and this was duly arranged. When we went up to the airfield on Michael's birthday, I was supposed to bring with me the logbook from the first flight. Unfortunately, with all the excitement, I forgot it and subsequently was most unpopular with the rest of the family, especially Fan!

Michael had his second most enjoyable flight. When they came back down and Fan wanted to pay for the flight, Captain McConnell wouldn't take any money, saying that it was a privilege and a pleasure for him to have Michael as a co-pilot. To mark the occasion and for his birthday, the Captain presented Michael with a coffee mug which had a picture of a steam engine on it. This was what the Captain drank his own coffee out of and he said he no longer needed it because he was going off to Saudi Arabia to work. He thought that Michael might like to have it to remember him by. What a gentleman!

When we said our good-byes and wished him good luck in his new job, the Captain gave Fan a kiss on the cheek and she vowed she wouldn't wash her face for a week, which amused us greatly.

I think Michael said, "You can't take her anywhere can you!"

In 1977, some friends of the family, Joan and Roy Priest arranged another treat for Michael. This time it was a visit to Manchester International Airport. Roy had been in the Police Service so, using his obvious connections, he was able to arrange a visit through the Airport Police Service. What a wonderful day out that was - I enjoyed it as much as Michael. His Uncle Bob came with us because Jim couldn't go that day and he enjoyed it too. We went through all the various departments of the airport, including the control tower. They got Michael up there in an ambulance chair. Then the Fire Department put on a demonstration for us, which was quite exciting. We were also shown around the Police Department. The Police demonstrated to Michael their computer connection to the Vehicle Licensing Department at Swansea and were able to show him how to trace the owner of a vehicle by taking the registration number and keying it into the computer. They keyed in the registration number of Jim's van and Michael was thrilled when his dad's name and address came up on the screen.

Following the visit to Manchester International Airport, friends and relatives suggested I write to RAF Cosford, which is quite nearby, to ask if they could arrange for Michael to visit there and, if possible, have a helicopter flight. Through my work at the hospital I managed to find a contact name and subsequently wrote to Wing Commander Tredre at Royal Air Force Hospital, Cosford. I hoped that he could pass on the request to the relevant quarters. He wrote back and told me that he'd passed the request on to Wing Commander Lobley at RAF Shawbury, where the helicopters were based. I then received a very nice letter from Wing Commander Lobley to the effect that flying was very strictly controlled and the rules were such that they could not, unfortunately, accommodate my request. As an alternative he suggested that Michael visit the Station at a convenient time, when he could have the opportunity to see different aspects of flight training and could see 4 or 5 different aircraft types.

We then heard from Flight Lieutenant Horwood at Shawbury who arranged for Michael and ourselves to have a guided tour around the hangars at the station. When we arrived we were pleasantly surprised to find that Ian Dorricott was also there with his grandad. We hadn't seen Ian for some time and although he looked well we could see that his mobility had deteriorated. While the boys were engrossed in the technical wonders around them Ian's grandad told us quietly that Paul, the younger of the two brothers, had died recently. The Dorricott family was trying to take

Ian's mind off the tragedy by getting him interested in things like aviation and they had bought him a CB radio that was the fashionable hobby at the time.

During our visit the Head Engineer talked to us and he was amazed at Michael's knowledge of aircraft and the very intelligent questions he asked. He obviously knew a thing or two about aircraft. We told him how avidly Michael read aeroplane magazines and how he studied the detailed technical drawings and did many drawings himself at home.

"I think I'm as impressed with Michael as he is with our aircraft!" he said.

By the time we were ready to leave RAF Shawbury Jim and I and Mr Dorricott had enjoyed the visit too and found it just as interesting as the boys had.

Shortly after Michael had left Porthywaen School, the White Lion pub at Llynclys got a new landlord and landlady. They were Des and Dottie West, who had connections with RAF Shawbury. When they heard from the locals about Michael and his interest in aircraft they were able to fix it for Michael to have a helicopter flight. All the children from the school, plus everyone in the village, came to see him off. He was even on the television news that day.

Gwyn Jones, Head Teacher at the Orthopaedic Hospital, assists Michael with some woodwork.

Chapter VI
'Murfee'

We mustn't forget another very special friend in Michael's life. That was 'Murfee' the golden labrador. Fan and Mick bought him after Candy had to be put down at the age of nine because of failing kidneys. Murfee lived at their house but, like Candy, he was Michael's dog. He was a beautiful puppy and when Michael first saw him he wanted him put on the tray of his wheelchair so that he could cuddle him. Murfee licked his face and made him laugh.

Murfee eventually grew too big to sit on Michael's tray but if we removed the tray he would very gently put his front paws on Michael's lap and stand like that for Michael to make a fuss of him, which he often did. He was a very gentle dog.

Whereas Candy had been an outdoors dog, Murfee was more of an indoor dog, although he did sleep out in his kennel at night.

When Murfee was about two years old he had a very bad accident. It happened one Sunday when Fan's brother Phil, his wife Audrey and their daughter Alison, plus Audrey's sister Muriel and her husband visited. As usual they took Murfee for a walk. This particular Sunday Jim and I didn't join them. They walked down the disused railway line towards the bridge at Llynclys and let Murfee off his lead. Suddenly and unfortunately he made a dash up the path to the main road and stepped out in front of a car. The car ran over him and everyone went running to him. I can't remember who it was that ran back up the railway line to let us know. Jim and I immediately got into the car and went down to the scene of the accident. Jim gently lifted him into the car, wrapping him in a coat. I nursed him in the back seat and he was whimpering quietly and shaking. He was in shock. I tried to keep him warm and could see a huge gaping hole in his side. He wasn't bleeding as much as I would have expected but after seeing that hole I didn't think there was much hope for him.

The vet thought maybe he could be saved and I held Murfee while he was given a pre-med. injection. Then they took him in to the operating room. One of the vets came out after five minutes and said that although his stomach had been twisted right round when the car went over him they thought they could repair the damage and save him but he would need a lot of looking after. What a relief! We hadn't relished the thought of returning home to Michael and the family with bad news.

Murfee was very subdued for some time after that but eventually became his old self again. He seemed quite healthy until he was about seven years old but it wasn't his stomach that bothered him it was arthritis! In later years he was to be a great comfort to Michael and to his grandparents.

Chapter VII
The New School

In the past I had always had a lift to work with a girl called Rosemary Peters who was also a secretary at the hospital, but before I could take Michael in to the hospital with me daily, to attend the special school, I had to learn to drive. I failed my driving test on the first attempt but thankfully passed on the second. Michael used to tease me and pretend to be terrified at the prospect of me driving him around. His first experience of my driving was in a Simca estate car. It was easy then to transfer him from the wheelchair into the car but as he got heavier it got more difficult.

Later we got a Cortina estate car and Jim did a very clever conversion job on the passenger seat to make things easier for me to transfer Michael in and out of his wheelchair. He made a sliding, swivelling device and fixed it under the passenger seat, enabling me to slide the seat sideways and swivel it to 90 degrees so that Michael was facing me. It was then easy to do the special standing transfer manoeuvre that I had been taught by the physiotherapists at the hospital.

When Michael got an electrically operated wheelchair, Jim bought a Commer van and converted the back of it, installing a hydraulic lift at the side door so that Michael could drive on to this in his chair, I would press a button and he would then be taken up into the vehicle where his chair could be clamped to the floor. Through Gwilym Jones, another friend at the Spinal Injuries Unit, I got the address of the makers of special clamps that are used to lock a wheelchair down to the floor of a vehicle, and ordered some. This meant we could drive Michael anywhere without having to get him in and out of the wheelchair all the time. We had a bit of a mishap with them one day though, on the way home from a weekend in Tywyn. We came round a sharp bend and I think one of the wheelchair brakes must not have been fully on. The centre of gravity shifted and the wheelchair tilted to one side, pulling the clamp free and causing Michael to bash his head on the side of the van. We stopped immediately. He was very angry and rather shaken up but luckily only had a small bump on his forehead to show for it. After that we made sure that the wheelchair brakes were always properly on and the 'quick-lock' clamps securely fixed.

The Special School at the Robert Jones and Agnes Hunt Orthopaedic Hospital was equipped with the same facilities as any other school and the four teachers covered the needs of the whole age range of the children, so that any child hospitalised for several weeks or even months (as many treatments for severe orthopaedic conditions required), didn't have too much interruption to their education. Having Michael accepted at the school was unusual because they normally didn't take day pupils. Mr Gwyn Jones taught Michael. He had a wonderful influence on Michael and was able to bring out all his natural skills and personality. They became great friends. It turned out that Gwyn had actually taught Jim when teaching at Oswestry Boys Modern School years ago and Jim remembered him well. The other teachers at the hospital school were very kind, particularly Margaret Stokes and Barbara Thomas, although they didn't actually teach Michael. Later during his time at the hospital school a lady Principal was appointed. Her name was Mrs Christine Peacock and she was a charming lady but she had more to do with Michael in his last years at the school when Gwyn Jones had retired.

I talked to Gwyn Jones a lot and he was always concerned with Michael's well being. He often had helpful suggestions for ways and means to enable Michael to do things for himself so that he could be as independent as possible.

Michael enjoyed attending the hospital school. Most of his lessons were held in the Children's Ward but the school did have a proper classroom which was used mainly for the smaller children. At lunchtime Michael would join me in my office where we'd have a packed lunch. My boss, Dr Francis Jones, always made him welcome and would chat to him whenever he saw him, as did his colleague, Mr Terence McSweeney, the eminent Spinal Surgeon.

Michael became a well-known personality in the hospital. He was also a patient, of course, having physiotherapy and hydrotherapy arranged by Mr Rose the Orthopaedic Consultant. After school every day Michael attended the Physiotherapy Department, where he was strapped into a standing frame to stretch his legs and prevent his hips and knees from becoming fixed in a bent position (contractures). This stopped when he became very overweight because his weight was causing little bleeds within the knee joints. Instead, I was shown how to do stretching exercises for his legs and I spent some time every day doing this. The hydrotherapy and the leg stretching exercises helped to prevent severe contractures for a few years, but eventually he developed some anyway.

At the hospital school Michael had the company of able-bodied children as well as children with severe disabilities. We didn't want Michael to attend a School for the Physically Handicapped because we feared he would meet other children with Muscular Dystrophy who might become ill and die during a school term and then he would learn more about MD than we wanted him to just yet. At least at the Orthopaedic Hospital School he would only meet those children who were having surgery or other orthopaedic treatment and who would be in-patients for a matter of months only. He made many short-term friends and met a few of the children again from time to time when they returned for further treatment.

A picture of excitement, Michael aged 10 prepares for his first flight.

Chapter VIII
The Yellow Peril

Working at the hospital again proved an advantage when, about a year after Michael had started attending school there, I came across a circular letter from Jeff Silk, the Sector Administrator, advertising the sale of a type of motorised tricycle car. A young disabled man from the Birmingham area who owned it had died and his parents wanted to sell it to any disabled person who might be interested. Back home I told the family about it and how I thought Michael would like to have this vehicle, especially for tootling around the sea front at Tywyn. He'd also be able to get around the garden and the street at home much faster than he could in his electric wheelchair and it would also be more stable, allowing him to go some distance alone in it. We tended to accompany him everywhere when he used his electric wheelchair outside the house. A bit of freedom would be nice for him. Everyone thought it was a brilliant idea so we raised the cash to buy it and contacted the family concerned, who arranged a date for us to go and see it.

When we arrived at the home of the young man who had died, his family made us very welcome. They were delighted when Michael was able to use the tricycle car in their back garden. It made them very happy to see someone else benefit and get so much pleasure out of their son's car.

Once we got it home Michael was a bit nervous of its speed at first but before long he got used to it and the 'Yellow Peril', as we called it, was soon a familiar site around Dolgoch where we lived. Jim added some gears to it and fitted a gearstick that was easy for Michael to use. We were able to take the little car to Tywyn on a trailer attached to the Commer van.

My Uncle Reg came home from Bahrain soon afterwards and stayed with us. He took several photographs of Michael driving the Yellow Peril. Reg asked Jim to go into partnership with him in a small agricultural and mechanical engineering business. Jim could do the agricultural work and Reg would do the mechanical repairs. Jim agreed and they called themselves J & R Engineering.

Reg lived with us for a time and shared a room with Michael. They got on well because they had a similar sense of humour. They enjoyed listening to the Goons on the radio and loved zany comedy. Reg would tell lots of jokes, could play guitar and sing. He kept us all well entertained and we enjoyed having him stay with us.

Later Reg bought a house of his own in Glyn Ceiriog. We took Michael to see it and we nearly had a nasty accident when Jim and Reg carried Michael up the stairs in his wheelchair to see the bedrooms and bathroom. Coming back down the stairs Reg was holding the bottom part of the wheelchair and as they came around a bend in the stairs he altered his grip, catching hold of one of the footrests of the wheelchair. It came off in his hand and Mike and the chair lurched forward, pinning him to the wall. Jim was able to take some of the strain at the back but it was a hairy moment and although Reg said he was all right I think it must have bruised him. He was only glad he had been able to save Michael from tipping out.

The Yellow Peril opened up Michael's horizons. We went for much longer walks with him than we would have with him in the electric wheelchair. It was nothing to walk three or four miles now. He used to like going to a place we called Sweeney Mountain because we had to go through a small ford. He loved driving the car through the water and would often turn around and go back through it again and again until we got worried about water getting into the engine and told him off.

At Tywyn there is a long walkway for about a mile along the sea front and he often accompanied us if we took a walk along it. He'd go on in front and leave us well behind. He'd get to the end of the walkway a long time before us and then come back to meet us, laughing and telling us how slow we were. It was a joy to see the pleasure this little vehicle gave him.

"No load is too large for the Yellow Peril"
Michael displays his zany sense of humour, posing in front of a trailer load of logs at Porthywaen Wharf

"What use is petrol when my battery needs charging?"

Chapter IX
Michael The Designer

By the time he was fourteen, Michael had become very skilful at technical drawing. As well as studying aeroplanes he now studied cars. Eventually he stopped drawing aircraft and just drew cars. He could reproduce any of the cut-away technical drawings to be seen in the various motoring magazines. We had a special table made for him at the Occupational Therapy Department of the hospital. It remained flat for him to read or eat on but the surface could be raked to about six different angles for him to draw on. He asked me to buy him one of those pencil sharpeners that you clamp to the table because these were the best and he was very particular with his pencils. He could just about wind the handle of it and we did it for him when he could no longer manage this.

At school Gwyn Jones helped him to make a proper draughtsman's 'T' square. Then Michael asked me to buy a special tool called a Flexicurve for drawing curves. It was a kind of heavy flexible ruler made of rubber that could be manipulated into any curved shape. He also bought several coloured felt-tipped pens. Thus armed he spent hours drawing cars. He had to support one arm with the other and lean quite heavily on the table, but he could use any drawing tool. The only thing he found really difficult was using an eraser and consequently would get the paper he was working on a bit dirty, but the quality of the drawings was amazing.

He became quite excited one day when reading Motor magazine. There was a competition in it to design 'an MG for the 80's'. He was determined to have a go at this and for the next several weeks his brain was in over-drive.

Michael made several practice drawings in pencil first so that the final drawing, done in ink, would be clean.

When Michael had finished his design he had to write a specification for it which I then typed out for him. This read:

'The MG concept is a sports car for the sporting, fresh-air motorist. Such a car would be cheap, reliable and easy to tune, with good performance, handling and comfort.

'This car is a 4 seater, 2 door, convertible coupe, powered by a 4 cylinder, 2 litre, double overhead camshaft, high performance engine. The engine has an iron block and aluminium head, incorporating hemispherical combustion chambers with a compression ratio of 9.5 to 1. The 5-speed gearbox can be either manual or fluid clutch with preselector mechanism. This is connected by a 3-point propeller shaft to the rear wheels through a limited slip differential. The suspension is independent all round by coil spring damper units with semi-trailing arms.

The steering is by rack and pinion placed behind the front wheels with the steering arms pointing towards the centre of the rear axle.

The braking system is by two pot sliding caliper disc brakes all round. The brakes are operated by a dual diagonal braking circuit. The master cylinder will have a fail-safe system.

The car has wire wheels with alloy wheels optional. The tyres should be low profile steel radials. Body construction is integral with detachable outside panels.

Interior

The seats are orthopaedically designed, with Dralon and vinyl (leather optional) upholstery and are extremely adjustable, including cushion tilt and height, back rest recline and rake.

The steering column and instrument pod are adjustable also, for reach and tilt to the driver's comfort."

The finished product was impressive. We bought one of those special hard-backed, large envelopes to send it away in.

The publishers acknowledged receipt of Michael's design very promptly and a few weeks later he got a letter of congratulation because the judges had given his design a 'Highly Commended' award! We couldn't have been more pleased if he had won. The first prize had gone to a professional designer. The number of entries for the competition had been 500! Michael's design appeared in Motor Magazine on 7th June 1980, together with the other placed designs and runners up. He was sent a complimentary copy of this issue.

Later Michael received another letter asking him to attend the awards ceremony on Tuesday 1st July at the Waldorf Hotel in London. He was very excited about this and so were we! It was to be quite an occasion.

As if this wasn't excitement enough, in the meantime Joan and Roy Priest, who had fixed it for Michael to visit Manchester International Airport a few years before, had written to British Leyland at Longbridge, told them about Michael's design skills and asked if Michael could visit the plant. We subsequently got a telephone call from Howard Goddard-Jones, Special Projects Manager, BL Cars Limited, to say that the Company would be delighted to host Michael and us for the day at Longbridge. He suggested a date and said that he would get back to us to confirm this. A letter then arrived confirming the visit, which was to be on Thursday 19th June.

We put all Michael's recent car designs together including a copy of the recent competition entry and took them with us to Longbridge.

We arrived at Longbridge just before 10 a.m. Then we had coffee with some of the Directors in the boardroom and Michael showed off his designs. They were very impressed. Afterwards we were taken on a tour of the drawing offices where we were introduced to some of the draughtsmen and women; then we were shown a very sophisticated technical drawing computer which they called a plotter and Michael was given some printout drawings to take home.

We had lunch with the same Directors who had greeted us earlier. It was a very nice lunch and we sat at the VIP table! I still have the printed menu today.

The most exciting part of the visit happened after lunch. We were taken to the Styling Centre to meet Rex Fleming, the Design Director, who was to show us around. First, he looked at Michael's artwork and was very impressed.

"We could have another Issigonis here!" he told his colleagues.

I tried not to show my ignorance, but I didn't know then who Issigonis was and had no idea he was the designer of the Austin Mini. Michael knew of course and felt quite proud of himself. Rex Fleming spent a lot of time with Michael, explaining drawing and painting techniques and demonstrating how mock-up, full size car models were made out of wood and clay. Every detail of style was included in these mock-ups.

Mr Fleming then took us into the prototype shop. There was a completed prototype of the new Metro, to be launched that Autumn, but Mr Fleming explained that it had camouflage panels on it to hide the true styling underneath because it wasn't yet ready for launching to the public and industrial spies might attempt to photograph it. BL did this with all completed prototypes.

"Would you like a spin in it?" he said to Michael.

"Yes please!" was the obvious reply and so he was taken for a drive around the perimeter of the plant. What excitement! Michael came back grinning from ear to ear.

"You can now say you were the first member of the general public to ride in the new Metro" said Mr Fleming, "but keep it quiet won't you, some of our executives haven't even seen it yet!"

We were also shown a prototype of the new 'Ital' model. The Metro and the Ital were launched later at the Motor Show in October 1980.

In a more secure section of the Styling Centre the Press were allowed to take photographs of Rex Fleming and Michael looking at car designs.

Praising Michael's artwork, Mr Fleming told the Press "I hope he likes my cars as much as I like his drawings. They show a lot of flair."

Before we left the plant Mr Fleming presented Michael with a very large framed colour painting of one of his own designs which had been signed "To Michael with best wishes from Rex Fleming, Design Director, Austin Morris and the whole of the Styling Department at Longbridge. 19th June 1980."

We saw some of the executives again before leaving and Mr Ray Bates, Technical Director, told Michael that if he could pass all his exams, get into College or University and obtain a degree in Automotive Design, then there would be a job for him with British Leyland Austin Morris. Ray Bates then presented Michael with a personal gift of Rob Golding's book 'Mini' inscribed "To Michael with my best wishes. Ray Bates, Technical Director, Austin Morris."

We were so proud of Michael that day and had never been so impressed as we were with the people at Longbridge. We could never thank them enough for what they did for Michael and for us. We had been treated like royalty all day by them, they had given Michael much pleasure and most of all great confidence for the future. He could now follow his dreams and we would do all we could to bring them to fruition.

We left Longbridge at about 4 p.m. We had been there six hours!

When the day of the Motor 'Design and MG for the 80's' awards presentation arrived, Reg took us to London in his smart car and brought his camera with him. He intended taking lots of pictures!

We were impressed when we were ushered into the hotel. It was very grand. The function room where the awards were going to be made was set out with stands displaying all the short-listed entries. Some excellent work was included, which made us even more proud of Michael's achievement. Many entries had been received from automotive design students and a few from professional designers. There were some very good entries by children and Michael was the only disabled entrant.

We met the Editor and other journalists from Motor Magazine and we talked to some of the other contestants. Looking around the display stands at the other entries, we got talking to one of the judges, Tom Karen from Ogle Design and we asked his advice on how Michael could become a professional car designer. He said this was quite straightforward. Michael would have to get a few 'A' levels, do a Foundation Course in Art and Design, and apply for a place at a College or University which held courses in Automotive Design. Lanchester Polytechnic was one of the best but Michael obviously had special needs that might prove to be a stumbling block for entry there or into a University. I knew of a college for the disabled attached to Coventry University called Hereward College and had seen one or two spinal injury patients accepted there, who also took courses at the University, so maybe it was not such an impossibility. We would even consider moving to the area if it meant that Michael could follow the career he most wanted. Mr Karen said that Michael certainly had a talent that should not be wasted and he wished him the best of luck.

The awards ceremony took place and afterwards there were one or two journalists and radio people doing interviews. Michael was approached by a young lady from some radio station but he was suddenly overcome with shyness and was unable to say much, which was unusual. I think it may have been because the young lady was very pretty!

We had a buffet lunch, which had been laid on specially, before leaving for home after an unforgettable occasion.

Michael had a very nice surprise later that summer when he received in the post a parcel which was very kindly sent to him by a Dutch young lady called Willemina, who had trained as a Physiotherapist at the Orthopaedic Hospital. The parcel contained a magazine called 'Panorama' and Willemina had written this message on the first page: 'See page 16!'

'Dear Michael,

I found an article about you in this magazine, so I though you might like to have it. It tells about your talent and about you being offered a job by British Leyland. Very good!

With kindest regards.

Willemina v.Rhijk.'

We didn't have a forwarding address to write and thank Willemina but who knows, she may read this some day and know how we wished to convey to her our thanks for the pleasure this gesture brought to Michael and to us. It made us extremely proud to see this article and we were also tickled pink to see Michael's photograph on the same page as Elizabeth Taylor, even if it was all in Dutch!

A year later Michael was still being remembered for his skill, it seemed, when a letter arrived for him from the then Design Director of Ogle Design Limited, Carl Olsen, congratulating him and enclosing an article about his company's work for Michael's interest. Mr Olsen had a personal reason for wishing to acknowledge Michael's achievement - he had a sister who suffered from a type of muscular dystrophy. Later, Mr Olsen wrote again to say that he was leaving Ogle and going to work for Citroen in France. Michael wrote to wish him luck.

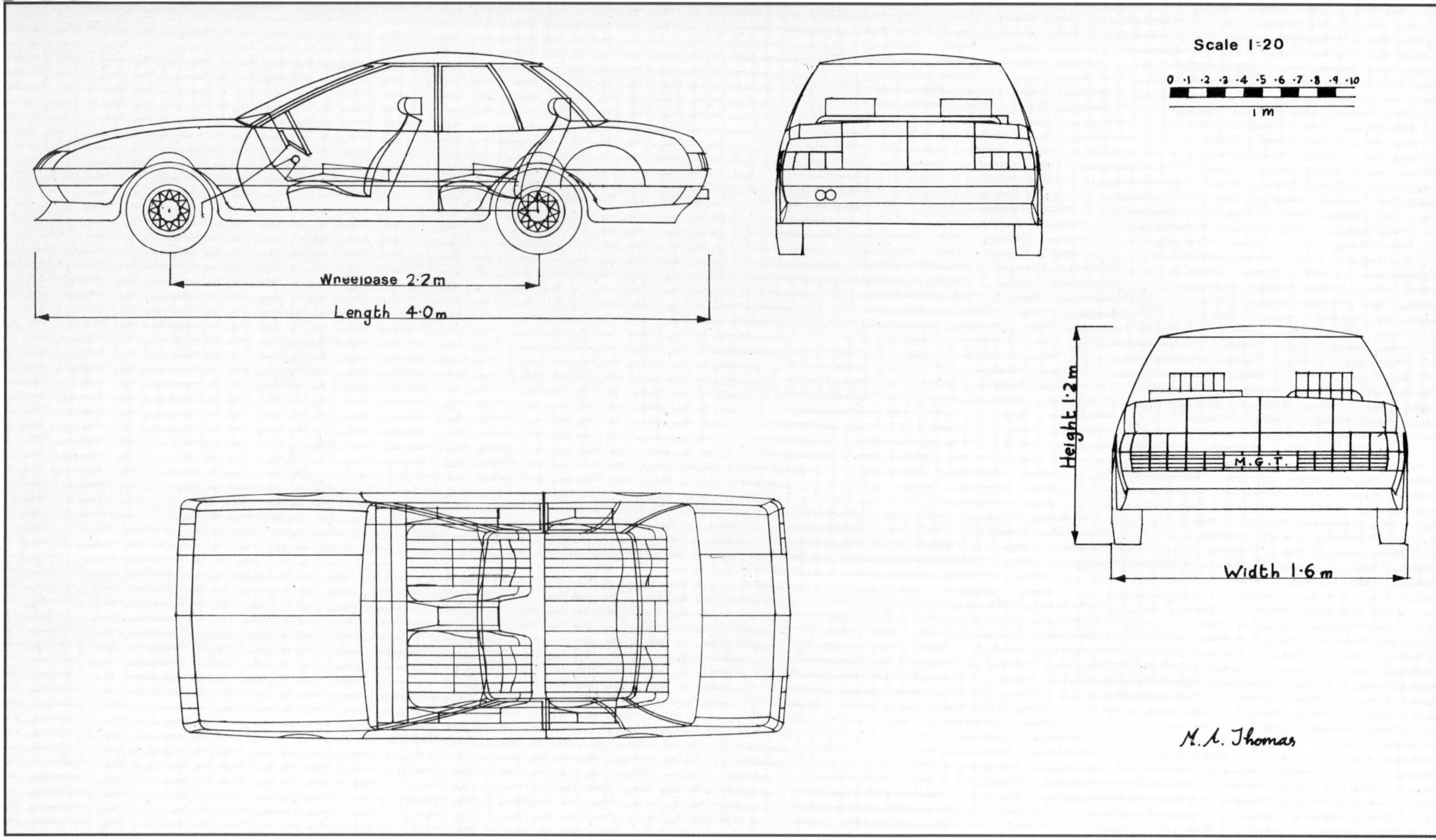

Michael's award winning design - The MGT 2.0

Motor

Design the MG of the 80's Competition

The entry from

Michael A. Thomas

has been judged

highly commended

by Tom Karen | Tony Curtis | Brian Hatton

Tom Karen FSIAD
Managing Director
Ogle Design Limited.

Tony Curtis
Editor
Motor

Brian Hatton FSIAD
Studio Manager
IPC Business Press

Motor

The certificate from Motor Magazine awarded to Michael

In July 1980 at the Waldorf Hotel, London,
Tom Karen of Ogle Design presents Michael with Motor Magazine's
Highly Commended award for his design competition entry.

Michael and other entrants from Motor Magazine's
'Design an MG for the 80's' competition.

Ray Bates, Technical Director, Austin Morris at Longbridge presents Michael with Rob Golding's book 'Mini'

Rex Fleming, Design Director at Austin Morris' Styling Centre, Longbridge admires Michael's designs and chats to him about them

Chapter X
Hope At Last!

From time to time Michael had follow-up appointments at the Neurology Clinic but nothing could be done to stop the progression of the disease. Over the years, as predicted, Michael lost strength in his muscles and, as orthopaedic problems cropped up, Mr Gordon Rose advised on these. Mr Rose authorised physiotherapy, hydrotherapy, special cushions or attachments for the wheelchair and other aids for Michael as and when necessary. It was a great comfort to us and we were very grateful for this orthopaedic support without which we couldn't have coped. I always had the greatest admiration and respect for 'GKR', as the hospital staff affectionately knew him. Having worked at one or two of his clinics I had witnessed his practical attitude towards severely disabled children and his empathy with them. But there is only so much that can be done for the many disabling neurological conditions which exist and we wished with all our hearts that some doctor somewhere would specialise in MD and be doing something towards preventing its progression, if not curing it.

Then in 1980, Gwyn Jones told me about a doctor called Professor Richard Edwards, who was the son of some friends and neighbours of his in Llangollen. Professor Edwards was based in London and specialised in Muscular Dystrophy. Gwyn promised to find out more so that we could get Michael referred to him. We were prepared to take Michael anywhere for some results.

By some strange coincidence, some months later, a circular went round the consultants within the hospital from Professor Brian O'Connor in the Institute of Orthopaedics. Being a secretary, I saw and read this circular which informed consultants that 'Clinics in Disorders of Human Metabolism would be held by Professor Richard Edwards (for Neuromuscular and Muscular Disorders) and Dr David Brenton (for Disorders of Calcium and Phosphatase Metabolism) on the last Friday of every month, commencing 31st October 1980.'

Referrals were invited. The circular went on to say that these two distinguished gentlemen were based at the world famous Department of Human Metabolism at University College Hospital, London.

This was what we had been waiting for! I made a photocopy of the circular and later showed it to Gwyn Jones, who agreed that this was the man he had been telling me about.

When I approached Mr Rose about referring Michael to Professor Edwards he couldn't have been nicer and he promised to continue keeping an orthopaedic 'eye' on Michael. He wrote to Professor Edwards and we waited for an appointment.

When we got to the clinic the sister in charge weighed Michael and, although we knew he was very overweight, we were shocked to find he weighed 13st 9lb - almost a stone for each year of his life. We would clearly have to do something about this and thought the doctor would surely remark upon it. We sat in the cubicle and waited.

We didn't know what to expect but just knew that meeting this man would give Michael some hope for the future. The curtains of the cubicle were drawn back and in walked this slightly built Welshman with a kindly face. He asked lots of questions of Michael, of Jim and of me, then proceeding to tell us what he was doing at his Metabolic Unit in London and that he would like Michael, if he were willing, to take part in a closely monitored weight reducing programme linked to some research they were doing with Muscular Dystrophy patients. This Michael gladly agreed to and we were all suddenly filled with hope. Here was someone actually doing something for this crippling condition. Michael was to be admitted to Professor Edwards' unit in University College Hospital, London on a date in the New Year, to begin the weight-reducing programme. During the weeks awaiting this date the family talked about nothing else.

Michael, having lost much of his excess weight,
sits out of his wheelchair to celebrate.
He helps his father run the bottle stall at a charity fayre

Michael presents Professor Richard Edwards with a cheque
donated to the Metabolic Unit at UCH from proceeds
of a charity evening organised by the family.
Sister Cooper (now Jones) of the Unit looks on.

Chapter XI
U.C.H.

We didn't have to wait long for Michael's admission date to UCH and soon we were on our way to London. Jim and I stayed at a B&B near the hospital. When Michael was admitted we were introduced to all the staff in the Unit, who made him feel very much at home. Sister Cooper was in charge of the ward; she was lovely, had a good sense of humour and Michael immediately liked her. Her staff were equally nice and this generated a happy atmosphere on the ward. We especially remember Varsha, a very sweet, gentle girl from the Philippines. She couldn't do enough for Michael or for us. The Registrar was a nice young man with a gentle and courteous manner. Maggie Lilburn, the dietician, was a quiet, charming young woman who was to make such a difference to Michael's life and to whom we became eternally grateful. Then there was the Professor himself full of encouragement and instilling confidence into his patients. They were a great team and over the next twelve months or so Michael felt he was part of that team.

The initial hospital stay was for six weeks. We took Michael in over a weekend and, as nothing would be done until the Monday, we were able to have a look around London. Jim and I stayed at a guesthouse in Gower Street, not far from the hospital. My employers had very kindly allowed me some compassionate leave in addition to my annual leave so that I could stay in London the whole time to be near to Michael. Jim stayed about a week and then had to get back home to earn some money. I hated it when he had to leave and I felt so alone in that guest house. I'd never had so many early nights or spent so much money on magazines!

Michael was prepared to do anything that Professor Edwards asked of him for the research trials. It was explained to him that before he could start the reducing diet proper he would, for a period, have to eat the same food every day. The reason for this was the necessity to have a 'marker' to measure his zinc and potassium input and output levels to discover a safe level of calorie reduction. Michael went along with this although he had to eat some foods he didn't like such as tomatoes. He must often have felt very hungry but didn't complain at all. Where he got his will power from I don't know because it certainly wasn't from me!

While at University College Hospital, Michael met another boy with MD called Paul Chadwick. Paul came from the Crewe area. He had a milder type of MD. Paul had been to the Metabolic Unit before. Like Michael he had a mischievous sense of humour. The boys had a lot of fun together and would tease and joke with the young nurses a lot.

It was a small ward and during the next six weeks we got to know some of the other patients. It was quite interesting to see the other cases there. Some of Dr Brenton's patients shared the ward. He had one patient in from our neck of the woods - from Pant. She was a young woman whose calcium levels had become depleted during pregnancy and after giving birth to her baby she had developed very severe osteoporosis and her spine had begun to crumble. She was in one of the side wards and of course had her new baby with her. The nurses made a big fuss of the baby.

Then there was Miss Dorothy Moreton, a delightful elderly spinster of about eighty. She was a real lady, an ex-teacher who had once as a young girl, she told me, taught at Bellan House Private School in Oswestry. She admired Michael tremendously and was very interested in his condition and the research he was taking part in. She enjoyed talking to him and to Paul and was pleased to have their cheerful company.

Miss Moreton had led a very interesting life and having lived out in Malaya for several years had been interned by the Japanese when they took the country during the War. She suffered from a tropical illness that had caused something like Ricketts. This of course dated from the cruelty and starvation she had suffered at the hands of the Japanese. She had written a book entitled 'An Irishman in Malaya'. It was written as a tribute to a fellow Prisoner of War named John Lowe Woods. The proceeds of the book were being donated to medical research so naturally I bought a copy, which she signed for me.

Another patient we could never forget was John. A tall, thin, very pale young man who was a little bit frightening to observe. He couldn't be still and he seemed to have big lumps here and there over his head, body and limbs. Sometimes he would lie on his bed, thrash about and moan in pain. It was distressing to watch him. The staff had to pacify John a lot when he was in pain. Sister Cooper and the other nurses gave him such loving care.

One day I asked Sister Cooper what was wrong with John. She said that he had a condition that caused these lumps to grow on his bones. These lumps even grew on his skull, which was obviously very dangerous for John, and he was a very sick young man. Michael was very sorry to hear this and was very concerned for him. Although he was a little bit frightened of John he made friends with him and tried to help him in whatever small way he could despite his own handicap. The two managed to converse a little in John's lucid periods.

The day that Michael was first admitted to UCH, on 3rd January 1981, he weighed 86.6kg. By the time he was discharged, on 23rd February 1981, he weighed 79.8kg. That was a loss of 7.2kg in six weeks and he was tickled pink. What an achievement! This, however, was done by sticking to a diet of only 600 calories! By his fifteenth birthday Michael's weight was down to under 70kg.

This was a crucial time educationally for Michael. Gwyn Jones gave him some set schoolwork to keep him busy during the weekdays. He didn't need any encouragement with his studies in Physics and Technical Drawing but he did have to be pushed a bit with his Mathematics and English.

Michael's school report for the Spring Term 1981 was very pleasing. In it Gwyn Jones stated: 'After his visit to London and as a result of his treatment, Michael seems to be much more active - both physically and mentally. Again this term, after returning from London, Michael has been able to attend regularly and has made good progress in all subjects.' The rest of the report read very favourably too. Michael was evidently benefiting very much from his stay at UCH.

The Summer Term report for 1981 was equally good. It began 'Again Michael has had a good term and he seems in a much more buoyant mood now that he is losing weight.'

Michael's weight reduced steadily over the next twelve months and during that time he was to pay several more visits to UCH. The second time that Michael was admitted Jim's Aunt Jessie very kindly put me up. Her home was at Brookman's Park in Hampshire. Every morning I would travel by train to London and stay at the hospital with Michael all day, making my way back to Brookman's Park at about 4.30 p.m. to try to avoid the rush hour. Jim would join me at the weekends, driving up every Friday evening and returning on Sunday evening.

Michael got on well with his fellow patients and the staff and was quite content to stay in the hospital for as long as was necessary. We took him out a little at the weekends but he wasn't all that bothered about seeing the sights. We did take him to the British Museum, though.

Because of the particular research trial that Michael was taking part in, before each subsequent visit to UCH, he had to follow a meat free diet. Meat or fish was substituted by eggs, liver or hard cheese.

In this research trial a number of drugs were tried, on a group of children with Muscular Dystrophy, to test several different treatments which were thought to be of possible help to the condition.

Michael and other children taking part in the trial were admitted to the hospital for assessment tests every six weeks so that the Professor and his team could follow their progress. These were mainly strength tests and biochemistry and took about five hours to complete. We also had to report any marked changes in Michael's life style, such as spending more time in bed or in his wheelchair because of colds, tummy upsets or other illnesses.

Because we had to travel such a long way from our home to London Michael was usually admitted over a weekend and was allowed home on a Tuesday. It was no longer possible to stay at Auntie Jessie's house but we were able to stay instead at the home of my mother's cousin, Ronnie and his wife Marge. My Auntie Stella asked them if they could put us up and they were only too happy to help. They lived at Ashford, Middlesex, which is quite close to Heathrow Airport. They were a lovely couple whom we had not met before and they took us in like old friends. We had many a pleasant evening in their company and they did everything to make us feel at home and free from anxiety. We can never thank them enough for what they did.

Over the years they also came to stay with us many times and we enjoyed going out together. Michael loved them too. Ronnie was quite a comedian and could tell jokes all night long if you let him. Marge liked to sing and was a country and western music fan so we tried to find places to take them where there was some entertainment, as they did with us when we visited them.

During one of Michael's stays at UCH Professor Edwards asked Michael and I if we could help him during a teaching session for his medical students by answering their questions about managing a child with Muscular Dystrophy at home. I felt the least we could do was agree to this but when the time came for us to go into the lecture theatre we were both very nervous. However, we did manage to answer the questions asked but were very glad when it was over!

Just before Christmas 1981 Michael attended UCH for a few days and he was discharged home on 17th December. It had snowed recently following which the weather had turned quite cold and so the snow had remained on the ground for some weeks. When we left UCH that day it started to snow again but we thought we would be all right and carried on going. The sooner we got home the better. But by the time we got to the Coventry area conditions were getting a bit hairy. From there onwards the journey was very slow and by the time we got to Wolverhampton conditions were very bad indeed and all traffic proceeded at a crawl. We were in a Cortina Estate Car and we were towing a trailer because Jim was doing a favour for a friend of ours who had a fruit machine business, by collecting a repaired machine for him. This trailer was impeding our progress even more, so when we got to a convenient spot Jim abandoned it. That improved matters quite a bit but a few miles onwards, almost in Wellington now, the snow was level with the hedges and people were abandoning vehicles all over the place. We managed to get into the town and I suggested that we try to get to the house of an elderly tetraplegic gentleman whom I knew very well, Jack Cornforth (nicknamed 'Cornflakes'), to see if he and his wife could put us up for the night. We found the house and Jim got out of the car. That was a difficult manoeuvre in itself. Then he dug all round the car and I helped him to get Michael out. He then had to carry him 'piggy-back' fashion to Jack Cornforth's house. The snow was up to our knees and was still coming down. I knocked on the door of the house and a very surprised Mrs Cornforth answered the door. She was rather embarrassed to find unannounced visitors begging a bed for the night. It put her in rather a panic. She hadn't been very well, they had very little food in the house and it was a very small house. She only had one single spare bed.

I said, "We don't care if we sleep on the floor so long as Michael has somewhere to sleep".

She heated up some soup for us and worked out some sleeping arrangements. 'Cornflakes' was quite pleased to see some new faces. He was bedridden, nursing a pressure sore, so he didn't see many people.

Next morning, thank God, a thaw had begun. I went out to find the nearest shop and get Mrs Cornforth some bread, milk, etc. Later, having had breakfast, we thought it was time to try and make our way home. Conditions had improved immensely and we got home at about 11.00 a.m. We drew up outside our house and were amazed to find half a dozen people in it! All were armed with mops and buckets, brooms, etc. and our faces fell when we went indoors to find wet carpets, furniture, ceilings waterlogged and sagging. Apparently our neighbour had heard a strange noise upstairs which sounded like rushing water. He alerted Jim's parents and they came round, let themselves in and found that a waterpipe joint in the bathroom had burst, swung upwards and the water was cascading up the bathroom wall and down again, flooding the upstairs floor and seeping through the ceilings into the downstairs rooms. What a mess! We had to stay with Jim's mum and dad for several weeks until the Council could do repairs and we could have the place redecorated.

We were given travelling expenses for each visit to Prof's Unit from a special Research Fund and when Prof later heard about our bad luck he insisted that we accept a further sum of money from the Fund to help towards any extra expenses incurred during our 'mopping up' operations.

Time went by and in less than a year Michael lost around 36kg. We bought him one of those funny 'Slimmer of the Year' certificates and he celebrated his weight loss by buying himself a suit in Oxford Street. I still have this suit today and the favourite shirt and tie that he liked wearing with it.

When he was fat we had to buy Michael special trousers with a pull down flap at the front to enable him to use a urinal bottle more easily. Zip fronts were just too difficult for him with his large tummy, trying to pee in a seated position. Now that he was slim he was able to wear zip-fronted trousers and he told us one day how he'd hated the flap fronts and used to wish that he could wear jeans like other boys.

Suddenly Michael was spending all his money on clothes that he chose for himself. In a very short time he collected quite a colourful and stylish wardrobe. Jim and I also tended to indulge him in his fashion whims, as did his grandparents. It gave us all great pleasure to see the new Michael emerge. His weight loss also seemed to make him more alert. This reminds me of the tee shirt he bought himself with, on the front, the words 'BE ALERT' and on the back, 'YOUR COUNTRY NEEDS LERTS'.

When Michael reached what was thought to be a good weight - I think it was 52 or 54kg - he was invited to take part in a further research trial. Basically, the idea was for a very low dose of anabolic steroid to be taken, at the same time following a high protein diet. The calorie intake was increased slowly from 1,000 to 1,750 calories, the protein being carefully calculated. It was believed that following this regime a muscular dystrophy patient would retain muscle for a longer period and could even develop some muscle. This regime seemed to have some success with Michael. We thought so anyway and, thanks to the weight loss too, he was able to use an ordinary wheelchair once more, turning the wheels himself, rather than using his electric wheelchair that was now only used for longer distances.

Transferring in and out of a wheelchair was now a doddle and at a fund-raising event in Porthywaen, organised by Fan, Michael was taken out of his wheelchair and seated on a bench beside his father to run a bottle stall.

I'm sure Michael had, at the forefront of his mind always, the thought
"I must do well with my exams if I'm to become a car designer".

Of course Physics, Technical Drawing and Art were pretty 'safe' subjects which he was good at but he really needed to work hard on the other subjects for his exams.

Once the research projects Michael was involved in at UCH were complete he settled down to his studying in earnest. In addition to his main studies at the Orthopaedic Hospital School he attended Rhyn Park School, St Martins, once a week for an art lesson. Rhyn Park was a very good local Secondary Modern School with a particularly good art teacher. The lessons were on a Thursday afternoon and I got permission from my boss, Dr Francis Jones, to take Michael there immediately after lunch and collect him later. This extra tuition in art paid off and Michael gained a GCE 'O' level as a result. In the summer of 1982 Michael also passed CSE exams in Mathematics, Physics, English Language, English Literature and Technical Drawing.

Plate 1: 'Flowers in a jam jar'
medium: felt tip pen

Plate 2: 'An exercise in Pointillism' -
Michael's copy of Seurat's 'The Bridge at Courbevoie'
Medium: Oils

Plate 3: 'A selection of food and other items'
Medium: Pastel

Plate 4: 'View from my Window'
Medium: Acrylics

Plate 5: 'The Horseshoe Inn at Llanyblodwel'
(a local listed building - the walls really do bulge)
Medium: Charcoal

Plate 6: 'Water Sport'
Medium: Gouache

Plate 7: 'Bedside Table'
Medium: Acrylics

Plate 8: 'A Winter Scene'
Medium: Water Colour

Plate 9: 'City scene at sunset'
painted from a photograph.
Medium: Gouache

Plate 10: 'A plate of fruit'
Medium: Acrylic

Plate 11: 'A view on the Gower coast'
painted from a fellow student's photograph.
Medium: Water Colour

Plate 12: 'A beach on the Gower Peninsula'
from a photograph
Medium: Pencil

Plate 13: ‘My bookshelf’
Another exercise in pointillism.
Medium: Acrylics

Plate 14: 'Big Apple'
Medium: Pencil

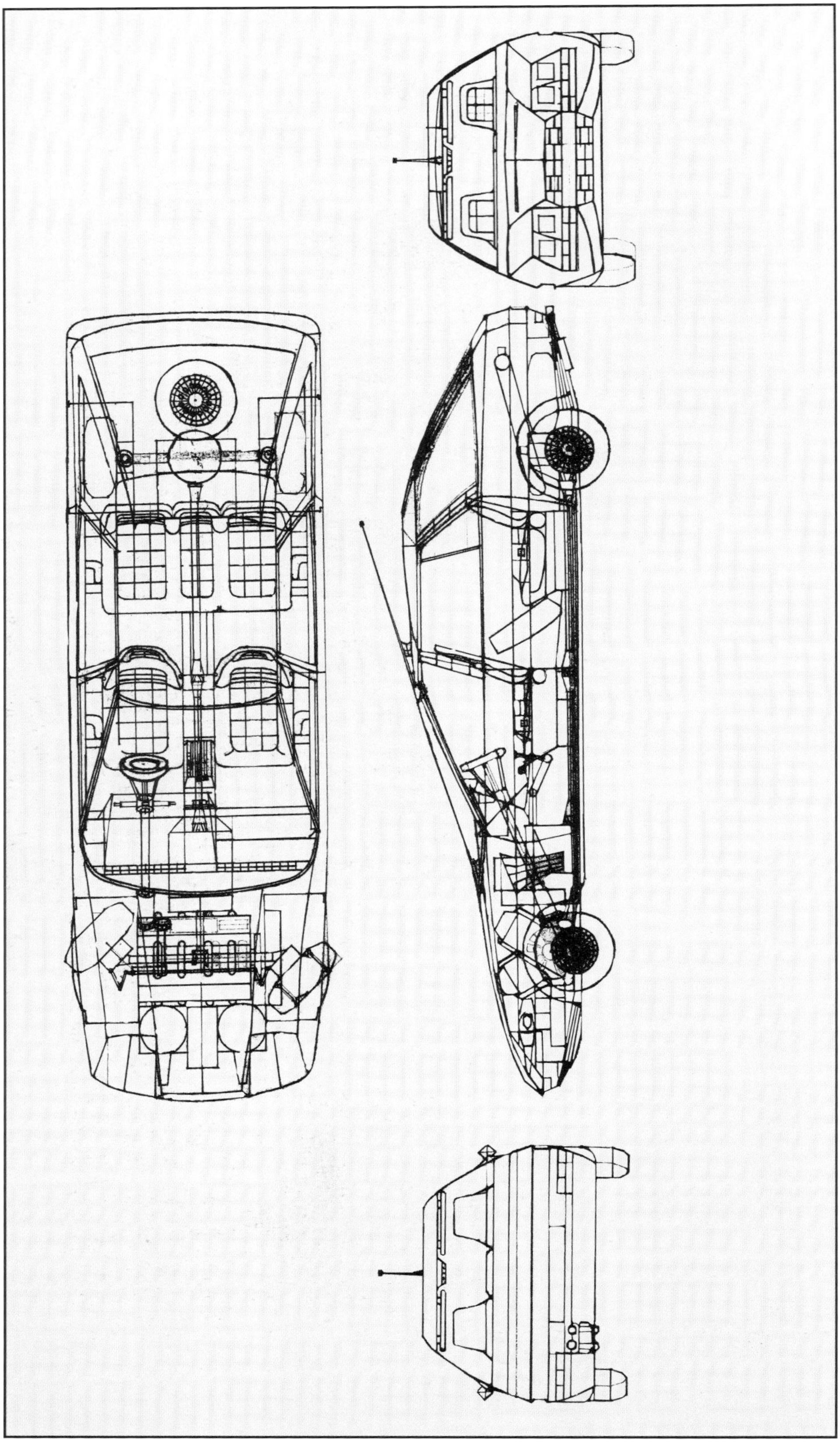

Plate 15:
One of Michael's many car designs

Plate 16:
Michael's entry for the furniture design competition

Chapter XII
New Friends

During the year that Michael was back and to from UCH we got him a CB radio. This was one of the best ideas we'd had. It was a good way for him to socialise and make friends. Jim's brother Bob ran a CB shop in Oswestry at the time and he was able to get a good one for Michael. Of course CB's were operated on AM in those early days and this was illegal, but such was the popularity of CB that the sheer number of users forced the authorities to make FM available to them. So, eventually, we bought Michael an FM model.

All CB users had 'handles' or nicknames. Most of these 'handles' were derived from the user's job or hobby or even the colour of their hair or their appearance. Jim always called Michael 'Fred Frog' and somehow this got changed to 'Tadpole' as a 'handle'. Michael's friends shortened it to 'Taddy'. He had many friends locally on air. There was 'Red Rooster', 'Super -A' and 'Tiger', to name but a few. But the ones who became lifelong friends were 'Muckspreader', whose real name was Michael Lewis, and his girlfriend Trina. Muckspreader lived in Maesbury and worked - you've guessed it! - on a farm. Everyone insisted that I should have a turn talking on the CB and they gave me the handle of 'Glow Worm'. I didn't make much use of it though; I was a bit 'air-shy'.

CB users could listen in to others on the air and eavesdrop on conversations, often joining in. I'm sure they had many a laugh listening to 'Muckspreader' and 'Tadpole'. Their conversations would be full of cheeky banter, jokes and stories of friends having fun. In other words, one laugh after another. Probably more time was spent laughing than talking. It would be impossible to measure the pleasure that CB gave to Michael. He even joined the CB Club in Oswestry and attended a few of their discos and parties, accompanied of course by his Uncle Bob (otherwise known as 'Moonshine'). Jim or I would take them in the van to the Queens Hotel in Oswestry where these functions were held, drop them off, and pick them up at the end of the evening. We would also take Michael's friends home and anyone else who wanted a lift. They would just pile into the van and sit on the floor around Michael.

Through 'Muckspreader' Michael met 'Swannick' (Russell Swannick) and his girlfriend Dawn and 'Sporran' (Duncan Morgan) and his girlfriend, Helen, who also became lifelong friends.

It was nice to think that Michael's teenage years were spent like a normal teenager, regardless of his disability. He enjoyed all the things that his CB contemporaries enjoyed. They liked him, accepted him, helped and protected him. What more could you ask of friends?

Using the CB one day at a weekend, Michael got talking to someone called 'Skull' from Wallasey, who was on holiday in the area. 'Skull' had a daughter called Maxine who was the same age as Michael and we invited them to call round to our house. Michael had his photograph taken with them. Their surname was Lennon (no relation to John Lennon!). Maxine and Michael exchanged addresses and promised to keep in touch. Maxine wrote to Michael while he was an in-patient at UCH. 'Muckspreader' and 'Swannick' would tease Michael about his 'girlfriend'. Maxine took up a nursing career and eventually the letters tailed off. I suppose she was busy studying and probably had a boyfriend in Wallasey.

Sometimes we would take Michael out for the evening with us. On one occasion we took him to 'The Tontine' a pub near the River Severn at the village of Melverley about 10 miles away. Michael was interested in the pool table and wondered whether he could manage to hold and use a pool cue. Jim chose a small, light cue from the selection available and after some trial and error Michael found a way of holding it that suited him and enabled him to hit the ball. An elderly man who Jim and I knew as Billy Lavender came over to Michael

"I'll have a game with you, laddie" and Billy introduced himself to Michael. They became firm friends.

Billy Lavender is a very romantic name, I think, and always conjured up for me the picture of a Romany Gipsy, which Billy was actually not. A bachelor, he originated from the Wirral, was now retired and lived in a caravan on land belonging to 'The Tontine'. It was easy to tell that he loved the outdoors by his healthy-looking, fresh face. His hobby was fishing and he particularly liked to fish for eels. The three of us had many an interesting conversation with him. He wanted to know everything about Michael and was impressed to know about his weight loss. He was pleased to hear when we talked about fish, that Michael liked trout and he told him about eels. He said

"If you like trout you'll like eels. I'll bring you one."

So we made a date to meet him again the following week at 'The Tontine' and he was as good as his word. I think he brought two eels. I was a bit daunted at the thought of skinning them, etc. but he explained to me how to do it and it wasn't so bad. I cut them into small steaks and put most of these into the deep freeze, grilling a few pieces, brushed with oil, for Michael and myself. Michael enjoyed his but I wasn't so keen on mine, finding the taste a bit 'muddy'. Although he had lost a lot of weight Michael still enjoyed his food and had an adventurous palate but he was careful what he ate. He liked game and would often eat rabbit, wild duck or pheasant. His grandad would often get him a rabbit and shooting friends who knew that he liked game would bring him the occasional duck or pheasant.

Billy Lavender played pool with Michael every time we visited 'The Tontine' and we often spent a happy hour or two there.

Chapter XIII
'Bovine Bovver'

Driving home from the Orthopaedic Hospital one dark and rainy winter evening, Michael and I experienced a rather nasty shock. Suddenly out of nowhere, this large bovine bulk loomed up at us and bang! the side of the van caught it. This happened near a layby opposite Old Port Farm just outside Oswestry. I pulled up as quickly as I could and, checking first that Michael was all right, I got out of the van. Two or three figures were running around with torches and I could see the cow in a crumpled heap on the ground, probably dead.

The farmer's wife came running up to the van.
"Are you all right?" she asked.
"Would you like to come into the house, you must be shaken up."
"I'm all right, thanks" I said "and I think Michael's all right, though it did give us both a nasty fright. What was the cow doing on the road? Is it dead?"

The farmer now came up and said, "I'm afraid she is. I think your wing mirror caught her in the jugular."
I shuddered.
"I'm sorry," I said, "but it certainly wasn't my fault".
"No, no" he said. "We took her new calf off her this morning and she's been in an agitated state looking for it all day. Unfortunately my father left a gate open just now and she found her way out and bolted onto the road."

"If you'd like to come over to the house," he added, "we can exchange addresses, etc. for the insurance."

I examined the van and there was a great dent in the side door, where the lift was situated. The lift was probably damaged and I only hoped that we could get Michael out.

"I think it would be best-to get Michael home right now" I said.
"Give me your telephone number and then my husband will telephone you this evening, report the damage and sort things out."

He agreed, gave me his name and their telephone number.

When we got home we were still a bit shaky and when Jim came out to unload Michael he was most concerned. He couldn't get the lift to work because the supports were buckled. Michael panicked a bit but we were able to get him out by making a ramp with two planks up to the back doors of the van. Jim was angry about the damage to the lift and how it would inconvenience Michael. He was ready to argue with the farmer if there was going to be any argument about liability. As it happened there was no problem, the farmers being reasonable people, but their insurance company was very slow in responding and it was three or four months later before the claim was met.

When I arrived at work the day following the accident, I was greeted with comments like
"I bet your deep freeze is full now!"
or, "Do you deliver your meat?"
and, of course, "Is it steak for supper tonight?"

Michael and I had many such comments made to us in the next few days once the news of the accident got around. It was quite amusing but I couldn't help thinking that we'd had a lucky escape.

Chapter XIV
The Operation

Michael continued to be followed up by Professor Edwards in his clinic at the Orthopaedic Hospital and each visit was like seeing an old friend again. A rapport had developed between us during Michael's frequent visits to UCH and by now Michael, Jim and I called him Prof, like his staff did. I don't think he minded. Prof would often have other professionals with him at his clinics who had come along to learn or observe. Sometimes there were distinguished people in the field of Muscular Dystrophy visiting from other countries. Prof would introduce Michael to them as someone who had persevered to lose a great deal of weight against the odds of immobility, who had achieved a great deal despite his handicap and who had been of enormous help in research trials which Prof and his team at UCH had learnt a great deal from. Jim and I were so proud when he introduced Michael in this way and we would come out of the clinic glowing. Prof had a wonderful way of making all his patients feel special.

I was very lucky in that my job at the hospital enabled me to call in at the clinic and speak to Prof between appointments if I had any worries about Michael that I wished to discuss. It was a great comfort to be able to do this.

In the summer term of 1982 it became evident that Michael's spine was becoming more and more curved despite wearing a brace and he was tending to list over to one side, especially when using his electric wheelchair. This was beginning to make his spine develop a rotated angle. In consultation with Mr Gwyn Evans, the Children's Orthopaedic Surgeon, Prof concluded that spinal surgery should be considered. They both talked to us about it and said they would like Jack O'Brien the Spinal Surgeon to have a look at Michael and consider his suitability for a new operation called the 'Luque' system. In this operation two titanium rods are fixed to each side of the spinal column with screws, to which each vertebra is attached by steel wires. Apparently this makes such a firm instrumentation of the spine that afterwards no plaster jacket or long period in bed is necessary as used in the past with other methods. In fact the patient is able to get out of bed as early as the second day after surgery, which is a very good thing in the case of Muscular Dystrophy patients, whose muscles waste if they spend long periods in bed. We were told that one such patient had already undergone this operation, which had been a success.

We had a family conference with Michael about the proposition of this surgery. He didn't like the idea very much but when he weighed up the pros and cons he felt he should follow Prof's advice so he agreed to the operation. One of the greatest advantages in his own mind was that he would no longer need to wear a spinal brace. The only thing Michael hated now that the flap front trousers were gone was having to wear a brace. He had a series of them; all bulky, all uncomfortable, but necessary. He was always thankful when it was time to have his physiotherapy so that he could come out of the brace for a time. When he came home from school he would beg to come out of it for an hour and I always gave in to him.

So Michael's mind was made up and it was arranged for him to have the surgery at the end of

July so that he could resume his studies in the Autumn for then it would be time to think about 'A' levels and higher education.

Just before Michael had his spinal operation in July 1982, we held a Charity Country and Western Evening in the Village Hall and raised £330, which Michael very proudly presented to Professor Edwards to help with the Metabolic Unit's research project expenses.

Michael was only the second male patient to have the Luque operation at the Orthopaedic Hospital and we were told that Eduardo Luque himself, the surgeon who developed the technique, would be assisting with the operation. Michael was admitted at the same time as a young girl with MD, named Liza Grzadzielewska, and they both were to have the Luque operation the same day. Michael's surgery was scheduled to be done first, but for some reason it didn't work out that way and they did Liza's first. Then it was Michael's turn and the following few hours were the most anxious of our lives. We knew that poor Michael was very nervous and worried about the operation and we were very tense about the outcome. Jim and I both went to work that day. Later that morning I found myself in the hospital chapel praying. I'm afraid it was the first time I'd ever been in there.

Things went without a hitch and in the recovery room later Michael seemed no worse than we had expected to find him after such a big operation. Next day he was able to return to the Children's Ward. On the second day after the operation, Vicky Draycott the Physiotherapist had Michael and Liza sitting out of bed in their wheelchairs for short periods. Michael found it a distressing and painful experience. To my own mind, although the safety of the spinal instrumentation was not in doubt, it was too early following major surgery to get anyone out of bed. Michael couldn't really tolerate it so after about ten to fifteen minutes he was put back in bed and they tried again later in the day. - It was more difficult and painful than he ever thought it would be and the rest of the week was a nightmare for him. For Liza it was no picnic either but she did seem to tolerate it a little better than Michael.

Michael was very uncomfortable in bed, too, and because he felt very unwell he got distressed and called the nurses frequently. Most of them were very sympathetic, Michael being well known by the day staff from his attending school on the ward, but two nurses on the night shift were not so kind. We always referred to one of them as the 'Gestapo'. Leaving the ward after visiting in the evenings we'd say to each other

"I wonder if the 'Gestapo' is on duty tonight".

Michael was so distressed following one of her nights on duty that we reported her to the Night Superintendent because of her attitude.

During that post-operative period Michael became extremely stressed and was prescribed some Valium. The only thing that kept him sane was the company of the other children. In the neighbouring bed, a Welsh boy called Robert was full of fun and he rallied Michael along quite a lot. Another thing that kept Michael going was the visits from his friends Muckspreader and Trina.

Somehow Michael got through the next few weeks. He had to stay in hospital a little bit longer than Liza did because he got an infection in the wound but this was believed to be clear when the wound healed and he was discharged home. I then had two weeks off to look after him.

He was a changed person. Gone was the happy, joking boy who was interested in everything around him. He had become a miserable, unhappy individual who had no interest in anything and who cried out with every movement he made. We were not surprised that his back ached or that he felt weak and we tried to make him comfortable but we didn't know what to do about his other problems. Not five minutes went by without me having to adjust his position in the wheelchair. He complained of terrible pain in his legs. When I reported this to Vicky Draycott she said

"Bring him in to the hydrotherapy pool, it will help to loosen him up".

One day we persuaded Michael to come out for a trip to Butlins at Pwllheli for the day. Fan came with us. The trip was a mistake, the journey tiring him dreadfully. He tried very hard to be cheerful but towards the mid afternoon he'd had enough and even became tearful. Looking at photographs taken that day, we can now see how ill and unhappy he must have been.

After about 2 weeks of hydrotherapy I noticed three long lumps appear along the scar of the operation wound and became very concerned about them. Vicky felt they were just sacs of fluid that sometimes appeared in long scars and she told me not to worry, they would either disperse on their own or leak and empty gradually. Sister Robinson, the District Nurse, was a little bit concerned about them and said

"We'll just keep an eye on them".

Every time I washed Michael's back those lumps looked more and more ominous. One evening one of them was leaking and I gently swabbed the fluid away. Next day when Sister Robinson called I drew her attention to it and she gently tried to tease some more fluid out so that she could send a swab of it away for testing in case there was another infection. She said I must let her know if there was any more leaking, especially if the fluid that came out was thick and orange in colour. If it was a clear straw colour there was no need to worry.

The next day when I went to wash Michael's back I turned him over and all three of what were now obviously cysts burst and this filthy orange coloured sludge seeped out of them. It smelt foul too. Sister Robinson arrived soon afterwards and telephoned the hospital.

They said, "Bring him in".

Poor Michael, he couldn't bear the thought of going back to Crewe Ward but it couldn't be avoided. Perhaps now those who thought he had been a 'baby' would be sorry to see how ill he was.

Then came the bad news. Jack O'Brien told us that this was a very severe infection. If it did not respond to another course of antibiotics they would have to re-open Michael's back in theatre and swab it out completely. However, if this happened they would not be stitching his back up again but would have to leave the wound open and pack it, allowing it to heal from the depths. The packing would have to be changed every three days, initially under anaesthetic, but as time went on it could be done in the treatment room on the ward without anaesthetic.

The infection did not respond to the course of antibiotics so Michael was then told what the next steps would have to be. He broke down and cried; by now he was in a very low state both physically and emotionally.

If Michael's initial post-operative weeks had been a nightmare then I don't know how to describe this second post-operative period. I couldn't keep away from Crewe Ward for long, I was so anxious of his progress. Jim and I were anxious too about what this long period in bed was going to do to Michael's muscles. The operation that was supposed to be the best thing for him was turning out to be the worst thing.

The dressings to his back were done daily after the first few weeks. The wound was packed from the depths upwards. I had the misfortune to go on to the ward one day when Michael was having his dressings done in the treatment room. I heard him cry out in pain and could do nothing. There was no way the job could be done without hurting him, I knew that, but it didn't help the knife turning in my heart. I had to run out of the ward and broke down on the corridor.

During this difficult time I was still working in the Midland Spinal Injuries Unit as secretary to the Director, Dr Barry Francis Jones. He was a very dear man. His patients and his staff loved him. When Michael visited my office he would chat to him and when Michael was having his surgery no one was kinder. During the catastrophe of Michael's post-operative infection he was a tower of strength. He became very concerned about my welfare and warned me

"Try not to go to the ward so often, Gloria, you are becoming traumatised with all this and if you're not careful you'll become a casualty also".

I tried to take heed of his advice but found it very hard to keep away. It was a very bad time in Michael's life.

It was round about that time, I believe, that we got the tragic news at the hospital that Professor Edwards' own son Tom, aged twelve, had been killed in a road accident. Jim and I were devastated to hear this and to think that this should happen to the child of someone who did everything he could to prolong the lives of other children. We sent our condolences to Prof and his wife, Eleri. Our thoughts were very much with them. I told Michael about the tragedy, which made him very sad.

Jim and I were becoming very concerned about Michael's comfort. It's not easy to nurse someone whose back is open all the way down to the sacrum and Michael went through sheer hell in discomfort of positioning, as well as pain from the wound. One day Gary Speck, the registrar, decided that Michael's wound would do better if he could lie face down. He was also concerned that fluid may be building up in Michael's lungs and felt that putting him to lie prone in bed could prevent this. To us, who knew that Michael's legs had by now become contracted in a fixed 'frog' position, this seemed impossible and we were concerned as to how they would achieve this and how he'd take to it. I arrived on the ward one day to find Michael very distressed. He was all bound up and lying face down. He couldn't stand it and he had got himself in quite a state. I talked to Gary Speck and he tried to explain to me and to Michael why he felt they should persevere with him in this position. I understood, but didn't like seeing him like that. I talked to Michael and tried to pacify him but to no avail. In the end I had to promise him that I would make them stop and find some other way to nurse him. At visiting time when Fan saw him like that, she made a hell of a scene. She called the registrar and the staff the greatest barbarians that ever breathed and demanded that they change his position immediately.

"What the hell do they think they're doing, trussing him up like a turkey!"

Michael was still very distressed and begged them to let him lie as he had before, which in the end they did but warned us that they could take no responsibility for the consequences. Then I had a brilliant idea! On the Spinal Injuries Unit they had a waterbed which was used to heal pressure sores and at that time it was not in use. I had the idea that Michael would be more comfortable on this bed. Many pressure sores had been healed on the waterbed so probably his wound would stand a better chance of healing more quickly on it. I spoke to Gary Speck about it and he said that if Dr Francis Jones were willing to loan the waterbed to them they would certainly give it a try. Dr Jones was only too pleased to help and we were so grateful.

Soon afterwards I came across another wonderful invention to speed up healing. My friend Rita and I also worked for Gwilym Jones, the Spinal Injuries Co-ordinator. What he didn't know about healing wounds and pressure sores could be written on a postage stamp. The surgical manufacturing companies were always sending him all sorts of bumph, leaflets and samples of new products. Sifting through some of the stuff on Gwilym's desk one day, looking for some information to answer a telephone query, I found a leaflet about a new wonder product for healing wounds and pressure sores. It was a special kind of sterile, quick-setting silicone which you mixed and poured into the wound; the silicone set to the contours of the wound but did not stick to the tissues. The wound was cleaned and the silicone replaced daily and, as with standard wound packing, the wound would gradually heal from the base but apparently did so much faster than with conventional packing materials. When I'd dealt with my telephone call I immediately marched up to Crewe Ward with this leaflet and gave it to Sister to show to the Registrar. They decided to order some of this silicone and try it.

The silicone treatment worked and Michael was able to come home for a few days at Christmas, by which time the wound had reduced to about 6 inches in length. I was taught how to clean, silicone and dress the wound and arrangements were made for a District Nurse to pop in daily to check that all was well.

Michael received a huge Christmas/Get Well card from all the staff at UCH, signed by everyone who knew him there, including of course Prof and Eleri Edwards. All had written special messages of encouragement and cheer. He was very thrilled with this. When I went into Michael's room later to pack his things, there were tears running down his face.

"What's wrong Mike?" I asked him.
"Nothing's wrong" he said, trying to control the tears,
"I'm just thinking what a lousy Christmas the Edwards' are going to have."

Tears pricked my eyes as I hugged him and felt proud that he was so sensitive to the pain of others.

Following our success in coping during the Christmas holidays Michael was discharged home in January 1983 and I had some time off to look after him.

Eventually I had to go back to work but I continued to attend to the wound night and morning. Fan stayed at our house all day to look after Michael and the District Nurses called daily to wash him and help with toiletting. Gradually he was able to sit in his wheelchair once more. Fan had one or two 'skirmishes' with the District Nurses because she was very protective of Michael and always anxious for his comfort after all that he had been through in hospital. For instance, if Michael was left sitting on the commode for too long, and became distressed, she would give the attending nurse a piece of her mind!

When I went back to work Fan or Mick would come over to the house and stay with Michael all day. Fan always came over to dress him and Jim would come home to help her lift him out of bed. Fan always worried about Michael's dignity and modesty in having to rely on others to assist him with personal things like bathing and dressing, so much so that she told me she always shut her eyes when putting his nether garments on. One day he noticed this and asked her

"Fan, why have you got your eyes shut?"

Without thinking, her reply was

"So that I can see better."

He roared with laughter and so did we when he told us about it.

It was wonderful to watch how the operation wound gradually closed up from the depths and when it was finally closed the District Nurses congratulated me, saying it was all down to me, but I couldn't really have done it without them.

Recently, 15 years on, the operation, performed by a different surgeon at a different hospital, was shown on a television programme that a friend taped on video for me. After watching it I now have a better understanding of the major nature of this surgery and what is involved. No wonder Michael endured such suffering when things went wrong post-operatively. I was, however, pleased to see that the boy who was operated on in the programme was only got out of bed when he felt ready, at six days post-operatively. Michael and his contemporaries were got out of bed for short periods two days following surgery. I had always thought this was too soon and perhaps I was right.

Chapter XV
The Sequel

Michael's troubles were not yet over. Jack O'Brien told us that a low-grade infection would always remain while the metal was still in Michael's back. The metal would therefore have to be removed eventually but would have to remain in his back for several more months before this could happen, to allow the bones to fuse. When we told Michael he was heartbroken to think he might have to go through it all again.

The following months were not easy. Michael's muscles had wasted a lot through being in bed for so long and we were sad that the good work done at UCH seemed to have been in vain. He was very nervous of sitting in his wheelchair and every little movement hurt him. He also seemed to have a lot of pain in the legs that was quite worrying. He was always glad to go back to bed in the evening and was not his cheery old self at all. His friends tried to drag him out of the doldrums but even they were unsuccessful.

This state of affairs went on for quite a long time. Then, in an attempt to cheer him up, we took him away for the weekend to Harlech where our friends, Tase and Jane, had invited us to stay with them in their static caravan. That same weekend Muckspreader and Trina and some of Michael's other CB friends also came along in a small tourer and stayed at the same site. In the evening we all went out for a meal at one of the local pubs.

It got a bit warm in the room and Michael asked me to take his jacket off. I went over to him and began this manoeuvre but as soon as I lifted his right arm he let out a shriek which was quite unnerving. Everyone stared at us.

"Whatever's wrong?" asked Jim.

Michael's face was ashen. "It's my back" he replied. "Something's snapped and it's digging into me. It hurts!"

"We'd better get you back to the caravan and have a look" I said.

Michael's friends were very concerned and he became more distressed when we got outside. He felt he'd spoilt everyone's evening.

When we got back to the caravan he wouldn't let me examine his back because he was afraid of moving. He just wanted to lie down. In fact he wanted to go home and we felt that perhaps someone should see him at the hospital but he and we were worried that he wouldn't be able to travel in a sitting position.

Jim had an idea. He said he could ask Muckspreader if we could take Michael home lying down in the tourer. Michael's friends had followed us at a distance because of their concern for him and in case any help was needed, so Jim ran back to them now. Muckspreader agreed with Jim's idea and between us we got Michael into a comfortable position on the bed in the tourer and I sat with him for the journey. To be passengers inside a towed caravan is of course illegal but if we were stopped we felt that the Police would be sympathetic. We set off for home.

We decided that the best course of action was to take Michael straight to the Casualty Department of the Orthopaedic Hospital. When we got there we explained to the duty staff what had happened. They brought out a stretcher, got Michael carefully on to it and got him out through the front window of the caravan!

As Michael was due to be admitted in a month or two anyway for removal of the metal in his back, the doctor on call got him admitted to Commonwealth Ward, which was Mr O'Brien's adult patients' ward. Michael now being seventeen was really too old to go onto Crewe Ward. This cheered Michael up quite a bit.

We arrived on the ward at an awkward time when day staff were changing over with night staff but the Charge Nurse, Mr Perez, got Michael put into an electric turning bed in a side ward, where he was to spend the next several weeks. It was such a comfort to feel that Michael seemed now to be in very good hands. His gran made the point that she liked to see male nurses attending male patients and felt that this would give Michael more dignity with regard to personal hygiene, etc.

The staff on Commonwealth Ward were wonderful. They knew all about pain because they treated patients with severe low back pain and post-spinal surgery cases. They were very sympathetic. They knew about the things that can go wrong following spinal surgery and about the pain suffered. Sister Judith Spragg was in charge of the ward. She and her staff gained Michael's confidence at once. He was given painkillers as and when necessary. When we went home after visiting we could relax without any worries.

Following a thorough examination by one of Mr O'Brien's registrars it was explained to Michael and to us that over the next few days he would have x-rays and tests and when all this had been done it would be decided whether the metal should be removed from Michael's back during the next week or two.

It appeared from the x-rays that one of the Luque wires had become loosened and the doctors felt that the sooner it was removed the better, so that Michael could recover quickly and get on with his life.

The operation to remove the metal work was scheduled for a Thursday morning but the weather was a bit stormy on the Wednesday night and torrential rain had caused some flooding in the theatres so all operations were cancelled for the Thursday morning. However, the operation was able to go ahead the following day. Once again Jim and I and the family went through a tense few hours. At work I again visited the hospital chapel to pray for him.

Later that day, walking up the corridor, I saw Mr O'Brien coming out of the recovery ward. I hurried towards him to enquire about Michael but unfortunately before I reached him he'd disappeared into the theatre offices. I was very anxious to know how Michael had come through the reversal operation and when I telephoned the recovery ward later I was told that everything was all right except that there had been excessive bleeding during the operation due to blood vessels being weak from the chronic infection. Mr O'Brien and his team had had quite a struggle stemming the blood loss. Michael had needed some blood replacement but was now comfortable. Later I was allowed to see Michael briefly, when he came round from the anaesthetic, just to give him some comfort, but was advised not to visit that evening so that he could rest.

I went home from work and we had a quiet evening. Telephoning the recovery ward before bedtime, I was told that Michael was comfortable but would probably not be transferred to Commonwealth Ward for a day or two. He would stay in recovery for close observation in view of his condition.

At 5.30 a.m. the telephone rang. It was Fan. The hospital had phoned her by mistake, frightening the life out of her, and they wanted Jim and I to go down there as Michael was not very well. She made us promise to telephone her as soon as we knew anything. As soon as we'd put the 'phone down it rang again. It was the recovery ward sister apologising for 'phoning the wrong number and worrying Michael's grandmother. She repeated the request for us to go down to the hospital. Michael was loosing blood as fast as they were putting it into him and was becoming very weak. They didn't know how long he could go on. Our stomach's turned over. We felt this was it, the moment we had been dreading for years. We hastily dressed and got into the car. We fully expected to find him gone by the time we arrived at the hospital but he was hanging on in there.

When we went into the ward I recognised the female orderly standing by Michael's bed. It was Isobel Tibbott, my mother's cousin. It was a great comfort to have her there and she'd only just discovered that this was my son who was so ill. She told me later that she had to be very strong and try not to think about who Michael was all through the night when she had been changing the protective pads under him as they became sodden with blood and how difficult it had been trying to hide it from Michael that he was bleeding so badly. Even the hair at the back of his head was matted with blood, which I had noticed as soon as we sat beside him.

Sister took me aside and explained that the doctor on call had sent off to Birmingham for more blood with a special clotting agent they hoped would work. The trouble was that his blood wouldn't clot because the vessels had become weak. He had been transfused with twenty-two pints of blood so far!

Considering that he might be dying, Michael looked incredibly peaceful and even smiled. Whether he knew how ill he was I don't know but he was putting up a good fight. We told him not to worry, he was going to be all right now that rotten old metal had gone, and before he knew it he would be going to college and passing lots of exams. We even joked with him. Isobel and the sister in charge tended to him in a most gentle, caring way while we tried to draw his attention away from the blood-sodden pads and pillows. Michael did not seem to be in any pain at all, which was a great comfort. Occasionally he would doze off for short periods.

Eventually the doctor came with the desperately needed special blood supply that had just been delivered and we left Michael's bedside while the new drip was set up. We went for a short walk. When we returned Michael had had all his under-bedding changed and had been given a wash. He smiled and said he felt better. We stayed a little longer until we were told that the crisis was possibly over and it was suggested that we return home to allow him to rest and so that we could get washed and have breakfast. I think I went in to work later. The clotting agent had stopped the bleeding and Michael's condition had stabilised.

Michael stayed on the recovery ward for a few days just in case he had to be whisked back into theatre or something. Luckily all was well and he was soon back on Commonwealth Ward, where his post-operative period was very much more comfortable for him than it had been on Crewe Ward following the original operation. He liked the electric turning bed once he got used to it and I only wish he could have had one when he was on Crewe Ward.

To be on the safe side Michael was put on a course of antibiotics following this second operation and when the course was finished he got his appetite back. The weather was also very good and his bed was pushed outside into the sunshine every day. After a few days of sunbathing he suddenly became ill and was very nauseated. We thought that maybe he had been in the sun too long. But then his skin turned very yellow. He had got jaundice. It was a reaction to some of the blood that was transfused following the operation. He became extremely ill and was put on a fat free diet for several days. He didn't want to eat anyway and consequently lost more weight.

Eventually he got better and after another week or two was able to come home. He was more cheerful this time but very thin, his weight being only 7st 2lb! He was also very nervous of being handled, transferred in and out of his wheelchair, etc. I think he felt that his back was now extremely fragile and he was probably right. Never again were we able to do the easy 'standing transfers', it had to be a two persons job to lift him.

Michael had been very unlucky over his spinal surgery but it would be wrong of me not to mention that many children had benefited greatly from having the operation.

Gradually Michael became stronger and happier and we were able to plan for him to attend Oswestry College in the autumn term.

Chapter XVI
Making Up For Lost Time

Michael was able to start attending Oswestry College in September 1983. Jim took him there and back every day. He couldn't have gone to a better place. We thought it was an excellent college and Michael was very happy there. They had some facilities for disabled students including a lift for wheelchair users and a Care Attendant. They even had a Co-ordinator for the disabled students. Her name was Judith Waine and she became an invaluable friend. Michael's first report in February 1984 was very good and we were proud that after such a bad year from summer 1982 to summer 1983, which put him behind with his studies, he had done so well now. He was the old Michael again.

In May 1984 he had his eighteenth birthday. Many of Michael's CB friends were invited to his birthday party. He even invited a girl he knew at the college called Lynne. She wasn't able to come to the party but she gave him a book of modern poetry called 'The Mersey Sound' by Adrian Henri, Roger McGough and Brian Patten, which he treasured.

Friends and family were most generous with gifts, mostly money, and when he totted it all up Michael was able to buy himself an Apricot computer and monitor.

What a night that was! At that time Jim was on the Social Committee of Morda Football Club and as such he was in contact with some booking agents for entertainers. He asked them to suggest something a bit different. We had ourselves already booked a small band of musicians. These agents suggested a man who played an electric organ with his nose and was also a bit of a comedian. He did a lot of charity work and would probably not charge very much as Michael was disabled. Anyway, we booked him and he was all right but unfortunately his songs and jokes were a bit blue and embarrassed us although we are pretty broad-minded! The band on the other hand was very good.

After Michael losing such a lot of weight and then having jaundice, we didn't want him to drink alcohol but that night it was difficult to stop him and although he started off on orange juice his friends soon had him drinking beer. He was slightly merry by the end of the evening but came to no harm and slept very well that night!

He sat some 'O' levels in the Summer Term of 1984 and got a pass in Physics and Technical Drawing. He wasn't quite ready for the Mathematics exam though and instead sat an RSA exam in Arithmetic, which he passed.

That summer, on 11 July a baby girl was born to Jim's brother Bob and his wife. Now Michael had to share his gran's affections. They called the new arrival Lisa and she was beautiful. Michael loved her and was given the honour of being her godfather. I had the honour of being her god-mother.

Michael was fascinated with Lisa and we'd often put her on his lap so that he could talk to her. Of course we had to supervise this because he hadn't the strength to hold on to her. He was as pleased as Punch to have a little cousin.

When she was older he'd tease her and pull faces at her. When she appeared he'd say "Oh no, its the little horror!" which he didn't mean, of course.

If we were outside he would pretend to run away from her with his wheelchair, but sometimes she would run after him. Lisa called him 'Taddy' like the CB lads did.

Michael's love of cars continued and he still wanted to be a car designer. He also wanted to drive and now that he was eighteen he felt he would like, if possible, to have a car of his own. It was obvious to us that it was physically impossible for him to drive but we didn't discourage him. We explained to him that disabled would-be drivers had to undergo special tests at Mobility Centres to identify what type of controls they could use. We arranged for him to have an assessment at Banstead Place Mobility Centre attached to Queen Elizabeth's Foundation for the Disabled. Unfortunately the conclusion of the Senior Therapist there was that "his levels of strength and pressure were too low to enable him to drive a motor vehicle." Michael was so disappointed and we could also detect his anger at this fact that he could do nothing about. He was very quiet for some time after that. I suggested to him that perhaps one day he might himself design some system that would enable him to drive.

That winter Michael became very depressed and we couldn't get him to tell us the cause. He just kept saying he was all right. It could have been something to do with realising that he couldn't drive. Either that or the fact that all his friends now had girlfriends and he thought perhaps he would never have one. Perhaps he was in love. Perhaps he had realised that his life expectation might be less than he thought. His old friend Prof brought him out of his gloom by talking to him about how so many people felt like this in the winter but come the spring they always looked at things differently. There was so much to look forward to, so many new challenges. He put some hope back into Michael's heart.

He sat his Mathematics 'O' level in June 1985 and passed. He also retook the Engineering Drawing exam to get a better grade. He had to work very hard but eventually got an 'A' in that subject in the autumn.

When Lisa was one year old, Bob, Carol, Lisa and her stepbrothers went on holiday to Butlins at Pwllheli. Jim, Michael and I went along too, as did Muckspreader, Trina and other friends. We had separate chalets. In the evenings Muckspreader and friends would take Michael out with them while Jim and I went to a show. Then we'd usually meet up with them later. We all had a good time and were sorry when the holiday came to an end.

I think it was round about this time that my friend Marion came to stay with us for a while when she was sorting out some personal problems. She was like a sister to me and she loved Michael very much. She always made a big fuss of him and although he used to pretend to protest when she hugged or kissed him, he loved it really. It was a pleasure to have Marion stay with us because she was so helpful and we had some good times together. Her life is more settled now but we still see each other a lot and go out together often. Her friendship has always been a great comfort to me.

Marion was Medical Records Officer at the hospital then and had a lot to do with Prof's clinics, making sure that secretarial back-up was available for him and that the appointments system was running smoothly. She took a personal interest in the clinic and would stop and chat to the patients. She got to know many of them, especially the children. If you mentioned the name of one of them she knew who you were talking about, the parents, where they came from, etc. and it affected her greatly when she heard that a patient had died. Sadly, at a later date, she left the Orthopaedic Hospital for a higher post at another hospital in Shrewsbury, but we still kept in touch.

The Social Club attached to the Royal Shrewsbury Hospital often put on some entertainment. Marion had heard that a band called 'Walk a Thin Line' were going to do a concert there and thought it would be something that Michael and his friends would like. The music was said to be very good so she booked some tickets and she, Jim and I went along to the concert with Michael and his friends.

We got to the Social Club early and watched the band set up their equipment. It was a major operation and there were cables everywhere. They had almost finished setting up and were testing the equipment when Michael decided he needed the toilet. None of us had been in the Social Club before and discovered that to get to the loo one had to weave their way through all these cables. Muckspreader said "I'll take you, Mike, they'd better shift this lot in a hurry or we'll run over their ruddy cables". And without more ado he made the band disconnect those cables that were in the way. This amused Marion very much and she laughed about it for a long time afterwards.

Michael liked music. He listened to whatever was popular at the moment. He joined one of those postal music clubs and began to amass a huge collection of tapes, records, CDs and pop videos. His favourites were Status Quo, ELO, Queen, Dire Straits, Phil Collins, Genesis, David Bowie, Eric Clapton and Simply Red, to name but a few. In the Christmas of 1984 he had been so affected by the plight of the Ethiopians that not only did he buy the Band-Aid record 'Feed the World', but he insisted on sending a donation to the cause out of his savings.

Muckspreader, Russ Swannick and 'Sporran', another CB friend, now took Michael out regularly. Our van was insured for any driver and so they took it in turns to do the driving. The ones not driving could then drink beer. When each of them had taken a turn at driving, I would then drive for Michael. That meant they could all have a drink. Sometimes the boys from Maesbury would deliberately contradict each other when directing me around the lanes where they lived. They would get me really wound up and I'd get cross with them because I could never remember the way to their houses and got very confused and lost.

Often, instead of going out they would stay in with Michael and watch a video. Jim and I would then go out and leave them to have a drink in the house. They'd bring their own beer and I'd make a few snacks for them. Sometimes they would bring one or two extra friends along. One such friend was Paul and there is a funny story to tell about him.

We'd had our bathroom altered and a special shower unit put in for Michael in 1985 and for a short time the old bath remained on the front lawn until it was taken to the skip. This particular night, the lads had come round for a night in with Michael so Jim and I went out with our friends. We returned around 11.30 p.m. to find Paul sitting in the bath on the lawn fast asleep and drunk of course. It had been raining earlier on and there was an inch or two of water in the bath. Paul's jeans were wringing wet but he still slept! In the house the others were drunk including Michael and they got a bit of a telling off! Then I took them all home. You couldn't be cross with them for long because they were such good friends to Michael. Recently Muckspreader, who eventually married Trina and they now have a lovely little boy, told me many other stories of some of their escapades with Michael and he admits that if we had known one half of what went on we wouldn't have allowed them to drive the van!

One bank holiday Muckspreader and friends asked if they could use the van to take Michael out for the day. I made sandwiches for Michael and everyone else brought their own. Trina and Dawn were with them that day. They'd stopped in a pub somewhere for a couple of hours, then they all piled into the van again and set off out into the country for their picnic. Michael always had a tray attached to his wheelchair so that he could lean on it for comfort while travelling. He already had his sandwiches on the tray in front of him and started to eat. One or two of the party who had drunk too much beer felt a bit sick so they stopped the van and they got out to throw up. Whilst they were throwing up Michael carried on eating his egg sandwiches unperturbed!

Another time when Muckspreader was driving and the others were all half-asleep, he decided to liven them up. He saw a newly ploughed field in front of him, the gate to which was wide open, so he drove straight into the field. This livened them up all right because they all had to get out, except for Michael, to dig the van out again. It was stuck!

"That's another fine mess you've got me into," said Michael, who was worried about what his dad would say. But he breathed a sigh of relief when the lads got the van moving again and we were none the wiser about this episode.

I was recently told a hair-raising tale, about how the lads had all got out of the van to spend a penny, except for Michael and they suddenly heard him shouting, "Help!" They turned round to find the van moving forwards downhill and they had to run like hell to rescue it. The handbrake hadn't been fully on! They were very apologetic but Michael was very frightened and swore at them. Later he laughed with them about it.

Michael had another friend called John Ankers. He met John at Oswestry College. John had been studying accountancy when he'd been involved in an accident, sustaining a severe head injury. After a long period of unconsciousness he underwent a very long rehabilitation process and when Jim and I met John I remembered seeing him before in the Physiotherapy Department at the hospital. I remembered watching and admiring his very patient mother helping him to get moving and walking again. We often saw them in the Department when I was giving Michael his leg stretching exercises.

John had made a miraculous recovery but was left with a poor memory and one foot and ankle that didn't function very well. He had several operations to improve his ankle, most of which unfortunately failed. Eventually, though, he was able to drive again.

John and Michael shared their taste in music and met to swap CDs every week. John lived at Welsh Frankton, a village that lies between Oswestry and Ellesmere. The canal was not far away from his house and I'd take Michael to meet John at a pub on the canal side called The Narrow Boat. I was able to leave Michael in John's care for a couple of hours while they talked music and state of the art hi-fi. The first time I took Michael there I wondered if John could cope with taking Michael to the toilet but Michael said that John helped him with that at the college so I needn't worry. John only drank shandy or squash so he was able to drive himself home.

Most Wednesday nights Michael would meet John and Friday nights he went out with Muckspreader, Swannick and sometimes Sporran and a few others. When Christmas Eve and New Year's Eve came round Muckspreader, Trina, Swannick and Dawn would take Michael out with them for a meal. Not a bad social life was it?

Michael passed some more exams in 1986 but didn't do all that well and was disappointed with his results. Earlier we had applied for him to go to Hereward College but were advised that it would be best if he did a Foundation Course in Art and Design first so we applied to Shrewsbury College of Art and Technology. They didn't do a Foundation Course but they did an equivalent Art and Design (General) BTEC National Diploma course. They required a portfolio of set art work for assessment before final acceptance.

Jim had a golfing acquaintance called Richard Bradbrook, an accomplished artist who had fallen on hard times. He lived on his own in a caravan and was quite a character. Richard came to give Michael some art lessons at our house. He was happy to have a can of lager, a few sandwiches and a small payment in exchange. Richard got on well with Michael and taught him some very fine techniques. The work Michael produced after each session was excellent. I couldn't believe my eyes when I saw his first picture, a still life of various items including a cabbage, some eggs and onions on a plate and tomatoes etc. laid out on a cloth. The way he had picked up the light and shade falling on these items was beautiful and that picture is still my favourite today. I knew he was quite good at art but the paintings he now produced would have sold anywhere. It was nice to think that if he didn't manage to become a car designer he had this wonderful artistic talent to fall back on. Richard had certainly brought out the artist in him. Shrewsbury College was pleased to accept Michael for the BTEC Course in Art and Design.

Before the beginning of Michael's term at Shrewsbury we bought a new vehicle to transport Michael around. This was a Morris 1000 with a raised top and we bought it from a disabled gentleman called Ken Williams who lived in Ellesmere. We called it the 'Pope-Mobile'. Richard Bradbrook took Michael out and about a little in this. One of their stops was the car park of the Horseshoe Inn at Llanyblodwel, where they both sketched pictures of this old listed building.

During Michael's last year at Oswestry College, I was at work one afternoon when a telephone call came for me from the Casualty Department asking me to go across to the department because my son was there. The attendant at the college had accidentally tipped him out of his wheelchair. This was very upsetting and I ran across to Casualty, finding Michael with a bloody nose, cut eyebrow, chipped glasses etc., but he managed a smile when he saw me. He was still shaking a little. The staff got him cleaned up; the doctor said he had examined him thoroughly but could find no real damage except that he was badly shaken and he might feel very sore for a few days. My boss allowed me to take Michael home and have the rest of the day off.

The attendant who had tipped him out of his wheelchair had accompanied him to the hospital. She was in tears and very apologetic. She said she felt very bad about it because she was pushing Michael's wheelchair along a tricky bit of a pathway to one of the outside units at the college for his next lesson. She was offered some help with manoeuvring the wheelchair but had refused it, saying she could manage. In the next second the wheels struck an awkward piece of paving, the chair jerked and out toppled Michael. Lots of people had come running to help put him back into the wheelchair but he was obviously hurt so the Principal had arranged for him to be brought immediately to the hospital. I can't remember the attendant's name, but she couldn't apologise enough. I was rather cool with her and told her she should be more careful because upsets like this could make Michael very ill. I felt a little bit sorry for her, but not much.

The next day Michael's hips were rather painful and it hurt to move his legs when he was handled in and out of his wheelchair. For several years his hips had become fixed into a flexed, abducted position and he didn't have the muscle strength to pull his legs together. The force of the fall must have flung his legs together and strained the ligaments. He didn't want us to take him back to the hospital and as he'd been examined thoroughly for any breaks we felt they could do nothing more. Only time would tell if any real damage had been done. We kept Michael at home for about a week but it was several weeks before the soreness settled down.

Chapter XVII
The Sleep Study

Quite soon after his fall Michael began to have trouble with his stomach and this went on for months. During the day he'd have very bad indigestion after everything he ate and would feel sick during the night, retch and heave and bring up bile. I had to attend to him several times during the night and we'd both feel shattered the next day. Jim would sometimes attend to him but Michael would always ask for me in the end so Jim gave up. Our GP believed he had a hiatus hernia and gave him the usual medication for the complaint. This kept it under control a bit in the daytime but as soon as Michael lay down he would feel sick. I used to get up in the night to him, bring a bowl in case he was sick, rub his tummy for ages and generally try to settle him down again for the night. Often I was getting up every half-hour to him. I couldn't help but wonder if the fall had caused all this. Since his operations Michael had had the most awful trouble with chronic constipation and to have a hiatus hernia as well was the last straw. I do believe he found these problems almost worse than the experience of the failed operation.

By now Michael, Jim and I were suffering from the lack of sleep. We were a bit irritable in the mornings and, God forgive me, I was often rather snappy and impatient with Michael during those weeks. At the end of my tether, I telephoned the Royal Liverpool Hospital, to where Prof had now moved from UCH. I asked to speak to him and he very kindly came to the telephone; he was always so approachable where his patients were concerned. I begged him to help. Couldn't he admit Michael for investigation or something? We were desperate. He said that he wished he could help but explained that he couldn't admit Michael just like that, for investigation, over the head of our GP. However, he knew that Dr Smith, his Research Lecturer, intended to call upon Michael soon to take part in some research involving sleep studies. If Michael agreed to this and if there was a bed in the next few days, then perhaps this admission could be brought forward. At least that would give us some respite and if Michael was unwell during that admission then Prof could contact our GP and liaise with him on treatment.

Within a couple of days I had a telephone call from Prof offering Michael admission to Royal Liverpool Hospital for a few days for an assessment prior to the sleep studies. The sleep studies would be done at a later date in Fazakerley Hospital. I breathed a sigh of relief and telephoned Jim. We both arranged some time off to take Michael to Liverpool.

When we had settled Michael into the ward, Jim and I went to look for some accommodation for two nights. We found a small hotel and booked in. Nothing much happened with Michael the first day. In the evening he started to have trouble with his bowels again and it was several hours before that was sorted. Apparently after we had gone he didn't have a very good night with his hiatus hernia either. The next day Prof came to do a ward round and came to talk to us. He then invited Michael and ourselves to follow him down the corridor so that he could point out to us where his Department was and where various other Departments were. He told us that he had arranged for Michael to have an MRI scan as part of the pre sleep study assessment. Jim and I were very pleased about this because we felt a scan would show up any undetected damage that may have been done during Michael's fall out of his wheelchair and maybe find the cause of his gastric problems.

When the second evening came around we went back to our hotel only to find that they had relet our room. In fact they thought we had scarpered without paying! There had been some misunderstanding and they had got us booked in for only one night. They were now full and couldn't help us. We were furious. We went back to the hospital to see if any of the staff knew of some nearby accommodation that we could try. The sister very kindly said that there was a small waiting room near the admissions office that could be closed off if necessary for us to sleep in. She would OK it with the security people and let us have a couple of blankets. The seating in the room was comfortable enough to sleep on. We were very grateful and tried to settle down for the night but we could hear a lot of noise around us and couldn't sleep.

At about 1.30 a.m. Jim said, "We could be home in just over an hour, you know. Why don't we go up to the ward, explain to sister and go home? We can come back about mid-morning tomorrow to Michael. We'll both feel better after a good sleep." So we did just that.

The next day Michael was to have the MRI scan. The scanner was situated in a separate part of the hospital complex. We took Michael there and they prepared him to go into the tunnel of the scanner. Unfortunately, because of his hip and knee contractures his legs couldn't be brought into a suitable position, even with support and strapping, to allow his body to fit into the tunnel. The scan therefore had to be abandoned.

Michael did not need to stay in the hospital much longer. It was suggested that his medication for the hiatus hernia be changed from Tagamet to Gaviscon, which was found to suit him better, and he was discharged home to await a date to attend Fazakerley Hospital for the sleep studies.

Soon afterwards a letter arrived for Michael from Dr Philip Smith, Lecturer to Professor Edwards, inviting him for a short stay of two or three nights at the sleep laboratory in Fazakerley Hospital. I was also to be accommodated in a side ward so that I was on hand to give any assistance that was required. The first night, before Michael could be set up for the sleep measurements, we had the usual trouble with his bowels. It seemed to take twice as long to attend to him because Dr Smith was waiting to set things up. Poor Michael, since his spinal operations and the long period of immobilisation, his abdominal muscles had weakened which made things worse. He experienced great discomfort because of pressure in his tummy and become very distressed when he couldn't relieve this pressure. At home we had to experiment with various laxatives and suppositories until we got results and sometimes we had to get the District Nurse in to help. Bedtime was always a nightmare because of this difficulty. Sometimes it would take two hours to get him toileted, washed and into bed.

Eventually we got him settled and Dr Smith, a very kind and patient man, began sticking skin electrodes all around his head and chest. Some of his hair had to be cut in order to stick them on. By the time all this was done it was gone midnight and eventually I retired to my room. I was awoken by one of the nurses during the night when Michael wanted to use a urine bottle. The nurse had managed to give him a bottle but could not put his leg pillows right to his satisfaction afterwards, so he had asked for me to attend to him because he felt only I could do this properly!

Michael hardly slept at all that night. He found it very difficult with electrodes stuck all over his head and chest, an oxygen mask, nose clips, etc., and was still a bit stressed from the bowel episode. It was hoped that the following night would be an improvement. However, next morning Michael had more bowel trouble. He'd had no result the night before and the pressure in his tummy was becoming unbearable. He became very distressed and eventually had to have a suppository administered. About an hour later, after a long struggle, Michael obtained some relief, but was so tired afterwards that he just burst into tears. Then he surprised me by begging me to take him home. He was obviously very tired and couldn't bear the thought of being 'wired up' again. I tried to reason with him, saying that he'd feel better later, when he'd had a rest. He couldn't let Prof and his research team down now, surely? Not only was the sleep study for Michael's own benefit, it was going to help lots of other young people with the same problem. That was to no avail. Then I suggested that I 'phone his dad and ask him to bring all his pillows from home and his own commode, even his own mattress if necessary, to make him more comfortable. He said that he would really rather go home but he'd think about it.

Before telephoning Jim I thought I had better put Dr Smith and Prof in the picture. Dr Smith couldn't be contacted because he was catching up with his sleep, having been up all of the previous night monitoring Michael's progress. But the staff did manage to leave a message at Royal Liverpool Hospital for Prof to ring them back and speak to me.

Prof telephoned the ward and I was summoned to the 'phone. He said he was very sorry to hear that Michael wanted to go home and abandon the study. Could I please tell him exactly why he felt that way? I explained about Michael's desperate tiredness on account of his chronic bowel difficulties that made him feel he would rather go home. Prof said he understood how Michael felt but could I please stress upon him how important these studies were. If he only slept for an hour or two the data obtained could be useful. They were not "playing about at research" here, this was a very serious study and had great implications for developing improved lung and heart function not only for Michael himself but also for other Muscular Dystrophy sufferers. Dr Smith had already obtained some important data from the first night's study. Then Prof gave me the disturbing news that Michael showed evidence of heart damage from sleep apnoea, which is a common occurrence in Muscular Dystrophy patients. Only from studies like these could treatments be developed to prevent further damage.

"Michael doesn't have long", he said, "but both you and I want to prolong his life as much as possible don't we?"

"Please do whatever you can to persuade him to stay", he said.

I explained to Prof what I had suggested to Michael about Jim bringing him his own pillows, etc. and he thought this was a very good idea. I thanked him for his patience and understanding and promised to coax Michael into a better frame of mind about staying. When I'd put the 'phone down the tears began to run down my face and I had to go to my room and wash my face with cold water to hide the fact I'd been crying. This was the first time I had really faced up to the fact that Michael's days were numbered. Until now this thought had been shoved right to the back of my mind. I composed myself to face Michael and persuade him to stay.

It worked! Carefully rewording Prof's message, I brought home to Michael the importance of his contribution to medical research. He agreed to stay if I asked his father to bring his home comforts. Hastily I 'phoned Jim and that night he brought the special pillows etc. to make Michael more comfortable.

On the second night of the sleep study Michael was much happier and he managed six hours' sleep which, Dr Smith later told him in a letter, supplied valuable data for the study. In his letter he explained the general findings of the sleep study and said that Michael would be asked to take part in another study during the late summer.

As things turned out further studies were temporarily postponed for technical reasons.

Chapter XVIII
New Experiences

We had another party for Michael when he was twenty-one. We felt he deserved it for all that he'd achieved since the failure of his spinal operation. This time we just had a disco for entertainment.

I remember my old boss, Barry Francis Jones calling at the house some time before Michael's birthday and, discovering he was coming up to twenty-one, he wanted to get Michael a gift. He saw that Michael had a CD player and asked him what kind of music he liked.

"Oh, I like all sorts of music" Michael told him.
"Do you like classical music?" Barry asked him.
"Some of it" Michael replied.

Michael wasn't really that keen on it but Barry seemed to want to buy him a CD of classical music. Just before his birthday Barrie called again with 'Handel's Water Music.' Michael's friends teased him about it, saying he was "going all intellectual" on them.

Following his birthday he had quite a good summer and was now eager to begin his course at Shrewsbury College. Jim was a bit concerned that taking Michael to and from the college would take two working hours off him each day and the business might suffer, so he asked his Uncle Arthur if he'd like a little job driving Michael back and to each day. Uncle Arthur was pleased to help. He was known to everyone in the village as 'Riley'. I don't know how this came about but it wasn't a CB handle! Riley had a good sense of humour and was always full of cheerful banter. We felt it would be nice for Michael to have someone like him around. We showed Riley how to manoeuvre a wheelchair up and down kerbs safely, etc. and he was quite confident about handling Michael. As for Michael, he was very fond of Riley and they got on well together. Because of lack of sleep Michael was a bit slow in the morning and I was sometimes disorganised and bad-tempered. I'm sure Michael was glad to get away into the cheerful company of Riley.

There was something new to report every day when Michael arrived home from college. He asked us to get him a camera and short tripod so that he could do the photography module of his course. He was able to operate a camera by using a pull cord. This was an interesting subject for him and one that he enjoyed. He found computer graphics interesting too.

Drawing from life was another new experience for him and he produced some good drawings once he got over his bashfulness looking at the nude models.

Then there was the History of Art and he brought home a list of suggested reading. The books obtainable at the college were limited so we had to buy a few. I became quite interested in the subject myself, especially when I had to test Michael on what he had learnt.

Since 1984, when Barry Francis Jones retired, I had changed my job and now worked at the Orthotic Research and Locomotor Assessment Unit at the hospital as secretary to the Director, John Patrick. I had some interest in the Unit because in the past, when Mr Rose (now retired) had been its founder and Director, Michael had benefited from the attention of the department's experts. Always an admirer of the achievements of disabled children and adults, John took an interest in Michael's progress and knew that he was doing the Art and Design Course. He had also seen some of Michael's art and design work and was very impressed by it. He told me about some friends of his who were design consultants and asked if Michael would like to be introduced to them. Michael said "yes please". John's friends were called Graham and Pamela Gale. Their consultancy firm was known as 'Galeforce'. They had just moved from the South of England to the Oswestry area and were based at Preeshenlle Hall, Gobowen. John put me in touch with them and they very kindly invited Michael to visit them one afternoon.

On the first visit Jim and I took Michael to the Gales' home. They introduced themselves as "Graham and Pamela" and insisted that was how they wished to be addressed. They made us feel very welcome. We had some coffee and Graham explained the type of work they undertook. Part of their work included market research. They made Michael feel very special and very much at home. We showed them some of Michael's design work with which they were rather impressed. Graham and Pamela suggested a future date for Michael to visit them for a longer period. We could leave him with them for a few hours so that they could talk to him a bit more about the design world, show him around Graham's studio and have lunch. At the end of that second visit Graham and Pamela invited Michael to contact them again if he needed advice at the end of his course or if he just wanted to keep in touch.

Unfortunately as things turned out it was the Gales who contacted us next about fifteen months later when they heard about Michael's death. At a later date we took them out for a meal to thank them for their great kindness to him. It was the optimism that friends like these had given him that had kept him going for so long.

Through playing golf, Jim had made the acquaintance of a local young architect called Paul Whale who was also the fiance of a friends' daughter. Jim told him all about Michael and his technical drawing talent. Paul immediately invited him to call at his studio and Michael went along for another interesting visit.

It was arranged for Michael's class at the college to go away to stay for a week on the Gower Peninsula to paint landscape pictures. Michael couldn't participate in this exercise but when the class returned he was invited to paint and draw from photographs taken by his fellow students. He brought two of these pictures home and they were very good.

Michael saw another design competition advertised in one of his magazines and decided to 'go for it.' This time the project was to design furniture. He designed a complete three-piece suite and coffee table. We were impressed but unfortunately this time he didn't get into the winners' list.

We have a friend called Brian Wilkinson, affectionately known to all as 'Wilkie', who does a bit of wood turning, furniture restoration and cabinet making as a hobby. Now that he is retired he does a lot more of this. He's a very relaxed, pipe-smoking, philosophising type of character and a joy to talk to. His wife, Wendy, does a lot of charity work with our local Muscular Dystrophy Group. When Michael designed the furniture, we were so impressed we said that we'd like the coffee table he designed made up so that we could use and admire it in our home, so we asked Wilkie to come and see Michael, go over the design with him and see what he could do.

Wilkie ended up making more than one table! We had one specially made as a gift for Prof, which he was delighted with when Michael presented it to him.

Michael and his merry friends at his 21st birthday party.

Christmas 1987
Michael (centre) celebrates at the Station Restaurant, Llansantffraid, with friends (left to right Trina, Russell, 'Muckspreader' and Dawn)

Chapter XIX
A 'Graduation'

In October 1987 Prof organised a conference at the Liverpool Medical Institution. This was the International Muscular Dystrophy Colloquium, attended by delegates from all over the world. The Colloquium was to be held on 22 October 1987. Prof invited Michael to come along and participate in his session at this conference where he wished to demonstrate the achievements of Muscular Dystrophy sufferers through lots of courage, determination and a little help. Michael was proud to accept this invitation.

On the day of the conference Jim was due to go away on a golfing weekend to Llandudno, booked some time earlier, so my friend Marion said she'd be pleased to accompany us. I was relieved because I didn't know if I had the courage to drive around the city of Liverpool without a co-driver.

It was all 'go' and chaos at our house that morning. Michael was very particular about his appearance. He could still just about wash his face and hands and shave himself with a little help, but of course it took longer that particular morning. He had one of these spiky hair styles and wanted me to do his hair just so, polish his pointed-toed shoes till you could almost see your face in them and check that the creases of his trousers were straight and his tie. Then there was Jim who as usual couldn't find things. I had packed his clothes the night before but there was always some last minute hiccup like finding a spare pocket comb for him, etc. and making sure he took hankies, spare shoes, enough money and the camera.

We got away at last in the 'Pope Mobile' and picked Marion up. Having done that we continued the journey from Oswestry. Things were going well until we were on the Wrexham by-pass when there was a sudden bang as one of our tyres punctured. We limped on to a petrol station a few hundred yards away and pulled in. I was a real novice at changing tyres and was very grateful to have Marion with me. We got Michael out of the van and jacked it up. The affected tyre was on the passenger side and Marion began to undo the nuts while I stood uselessly by. Suddenly a fleet of cars went past, the passengers hooting, shouting and waving. It was the golfing party! They didn't stop because they couldn't see Marion stooping the other side of the van trying to get the tyre off and couldn't tell that the car was jacked up. They didn't realise we had a problem. They thought we had just stopped for a break!

Michael swore. He got in quite a temper because he knew he would now be late for his 'spot' at the Conference and was disappointed to have let Prof down. Michael was able to laugh about it later and for a long time afterwards would tease his father about that day when the golfing party left us to fend for ourselves.

The tyre changed, we then tried to telephone a message through to Prof at the Liverpool Medical Institution, but we had difficulty getting through and had to abandon it. We decided to continue the journey and explain when we got there. Michael was very disgruntled and disappointed with our progress so far.

At the Liverpool Medical Institution we arrived during the coffee interval of the Colloquium. We found Prof, who immediately came forward when he saw us approaching.

"Thank God you're all right" he said.
"I was worried about you but I knew Michael wouldn't let me down if he could help it".

I explained about the puncture and he was sorry about our bad luck. Prof was delighted to see that Marion was with us and greeted her with great affection. He introduced the three of us to his colleagues and then to Michael he said, "We've juggled things around a bit, so we can still fit you in"

Later, when we were ushered into the lecture theatre, Prof introduced Michael to the audience and talked about his successful weight reduction, failed spinal surgery, helpful participation in the sleep study, etc., but most of all, his artistic and design talents. Then Prof suggested that I hand Michael's artwork around the audience so that all the participants in the Colloquium could appreciate his talent. They did appreciate it and asked him lots of questions about his work. They also wanted to know how it was possible for him to physically manage to paint and draw. I explained how he had enough power in his hands and fingers to hold a pencil or brush but he had to support his working arm with his other arm to prevent it from tiring too quickly. It took a lot of effort and patience for him to produce the finished work. It also tired him quite a bit.

When they'd finished talking to Michael he was loudly applauded. Prof then produced a parcel, which he presented to Michael as a 'thank you' gift for contributing to the Colloquium and for all his co-operation with research projects over the years. Michael was quite taken aback. Marion and I were very moved by Prof's gesture. I knew that Michael would probably never get into a college or university but as far as I was concerned this day was his graduation and I was sorry that Jim had missed it.

Prof's gift was a wonderful Readers Digest book entitled 'Marvels and Mysteries of the World Around Us'. He knew about Michael's interest in Physics and felt he would appreciate such a book. The inscription inside read 'For Michael Thomas with many thanks and admiration from Richard Edwards. To remember your visit to the Liverpool Medical Institution to take part in the International Muscular Dystrophy Colloquium, 22nd October 1987.' A special photograph was taken of this presentation and Prof later sent us two copies of it, one of which has been proudly displayed at home ever since.

Chapter XX
The Big Disappointment

Michael did very well during the first year of the BTEC course. He got a pass in the Media Studies, Design Studies and Complementary Studies modules, a Sketchbook pass and a Merit in Fine Art Studies. At the bottom of his end of year report, though, the Tutor's Comment must have been like a great slap in the face. It read 'Michael has worked well this year and made good progress. It is unfortunate the college does not have the staffing and resources required for Michael to participate fully in Stage II of the course. I would like to wish Michael every success in the future.'

He was inconsolable. He was quiet for days. We were angry at the college authorities. When they had interviewed Michael initially they had been quite confident that they could cope with him. We felt that the real reason they couldn't take him on for the second year was that they couldn't be bothered to find ways to cope with his difficulties when there were other places who perhaps could. At the hospital I had seen how the disabled, with a little assistance, ingenuity and gadgetry, had been enabled to do things. I couldn't believe the college had given up on Michael. Oswestry College wouldn't have done so. That was it! We cheered Michael up a little by promising to arrange for him to go to Oswestry College again. They surely had some art or design course that he could continue there. As soon as there was someone at the college before the start of the next term we would arrange this for him. At this suggestion he tried to put on a brave face but I knew in my heart of hearts that his dream was gone. Jim and I were so angry and hurt for him that we wrote to the Principal at Shrewsbury but all he could say was he understood that Michael could not use any of the equipment at the college.

During the summer holidays Michael seemed tired all the time. He was awake most of the night every night. If he wasn't needing assisted coughing, or feeling sick with the hiatus hernia, he was uncomfortable, especially with his head and neck.

I tried all sorts of different pillows. One night, suffering myself from lack of sleep, having got up to him every half an hour, I'm ashamed to say I lost my patience with the pillows, lost my temper, shouted, cursed, and threw the pillows on the floor.

Jim shouted from the next room, "What the hell's going on?"
Michael was bewildered and distressed by my behaviour and I was very sorry.
"I'm just frustrated about these pillows and not being able to get them right," I said.
"I'm sorry Michael, I'm not cross with you".
I hugged him tightly and he said "It's all right, I forgive you mum."
But I couldn't forgive myself.

That summer Michael caught quite a few colds. The weather was not very good and when he did go out with the lads I worried that he wasn't dressed warmly enough and was terrified of him getting a chest infection. He did get one and needed frequent assisted coughing, as shown by the physiotherapists, and postural drainage by tipping the bottom of the bed up. A physiotherapist friend of mine from the hospital, Bobbie Mansell, who lived a couple of miles away, very kindly came to help on several occasions.

Michael also had some sinus trouble and found it helpful to inhale Olbas Oil with a steaming bowl in front of him and a towel over his head.

His bowel problem now became worse than ever. The only time he felt really sorry for himself was when he was sitting on the loo. He was brave about everything else.

He was so tired he would ask for a cushion or a pillow to be put on the tray attached to his wheelchair so that he could have 'forty winks'. One day I looked up from a book I was reading to find him nodding off leaning on a kitchen roll. That really upset me but I tried not to show it.

The time came for him to start attending Oswestry College again for the new course. I worried as to whether he was really well enough but he rallied round and was eager to start.

When he began the new course it was found that one of the pieces of equipment there, a lathe, was impossible for him to use even with assistance. However it was suggested that a miniature version of the lathe would be useable, or would be adaptable for use within minimum assistance, be someone as disabled as Michael. It was further suggested that we might consider buying such a lathe ourselves so that Michael could perhaps use it for a hobby at home. Jim talked to Mike Lopez, one of the Lecturers, about this. He pointed out to Jim one or two makes of mini-lathes in some industrial machinery catalogues that he had. Jim contacted a firm in Warrington for some up-to-date literature and price lists.

Soon afterwards I was talking to Karen Jones from our local Muscular Dystrophy Group about it and she suggested that the Group might consider buying this mini-lathe for Michael from their local charity fund. The fund hadn't been used recently and she felt sure that the Committee would be only too pleased to help. In a very short space of time after I spoke to Karen she telephoned us to tell us to go ahead and buy the lathe, the cost of which would then be reimbursed by the Group. We were extremely grateful to the Group for their kind help. Jim immediately telephoned the company in Warrington and placed an order for the lathe, collecting it a week or two later. Michael was now all set for every aspect of his new course.

Little did we know that only weeks later we would be presenting this lathe to the College, for use by other disabled students, in memory of Michael. At this presentation we were very moved when we ourselves were presented with a framed drawing of Michael, done by a profoundly deaf fellow art student named Karen Chatterton.

Chapter XXI
Time Runs Out

Michael had only been at the college a couple of weeks, when he seemed to get another chest infection and had to have a week off. Again he rallied round, went back to college, and even went out with his friends on the Friday evening. However, the next morning he seemed to want to cough something up all the time but couldn't and I couldn't seem to do any good with the assisted coughing, etc. I debated with myself whether to call on Bobbie Mansell again, but instead persevered with my own efforts. I didn't bother to go shopping that day and carried on trying to help Michael cough for the rest of the day. In fact I telephoned the surgery and asked for the services of the Community Physiotherapist, who they said they would send as soon as possible.

By the Saturday evening Michael was quite tired but when bedtime came his chest seemed to get tighter and tighter. He hated having the bed tipped and eventually asked Jim and I to get him out of bed and into his chair, later refusing to be put to bed again. I sat with him in his room, occasionally helping him to cough.

By about 3 a.m. it was becoming clear to me that he may be developing pneumonia so I suggested that perhaps we should call the family doctor. After some argument Michael agreed. I felt that if a doctor saw him he would admit him to hospital where Michael would benefit from the attention of a physiotherapist. On the telephone to the doctor on call, Dr John, I told him that I felt Michael should be in hospital and was sure that he would agree when he had seen him. Dr John came to see him and after examining him he got on the telephone to the Royal Shrewsbury Hospital. I overheard his conversation, which was basically telling the hospital that here was a severely disabled young man with Muscular Dystrophy who had possible impending respiratory failure and should be admitted. It was then about 4.30 a.m. The ambulance arrived soon afterwards.

I travelled with Michael in the ambulance and Jim followed in the car. Michael was given some oxygen during the journey. He smiled at me but was obviously frightened.

We arrived at the hospital and were surprised to find that he was being admitted to a general ward, not the Intensive Care Unit. But perhaps, we thought, they felt he wasn't ill enough for that, which made us feel a little less worried.

On the ward the nursing staff obviously wanted to get Michael into a bed to be examined but for reasons known only to himself, Michael protested about this.

We told him "You can't be examined properly unless you're in bed. How can they start treating you until you've been examined?"

In the end he agreed and, although I had explained to the staff that they must support his legs at all times to prevent them flopping open because of his useless muscles, he was extremely agitated and nervous and made rather a lot of noise. After the examination by a young Houseman, he begged to be got out of bed again, pleading

"Please, please get me up in the chair."

But he wouldn't explain why he couldn't tolerate being in bed. He'd had no sleep all night and must have been exhausted. We were pretty exhausted ourselves. We surmised later that when Michael was put to lie down he must have had a frightening feeling in the chest and thought he would die if he stayed there. Sitting in his chair must have relieved this feeling.

Following Michael's examination by the Houseman we were told that no real treatment could begin until the Chest Specialist had seen him, which would be later in the day. In the meantime the Physiotherapist would have a look at him during the morning and would advise and instruct us accordingly.

We waited and we waited. I continued doing assisted coughing on Michael intermittently but nothing came of it. We couldn't do any 'tipping up' because he wouldn't allow us to put him on the bed.

At breakfast Michael said he would try and eat a bowl of Cornflakes but failed after one mouthful. It was rather warm on the ward and Michael seemed to be having bouts of profuse sweating. He asked to be taken out on to the corridor to cool off so we did this. I lost count of the times he had to be taken into the corridor that day in between assisted coughing sessions.

Still we waited for the Physiotherapist. Jim said he would go home, have a shower and change of clothes and get something to eat. He would then bring back with him the commode chair that Michael preferred to use, should he need it. When Jim returned and once the Physiotherapist had been, I would then go home for an hour to freshen up and have a snack. We had already taken it in turns to have a cup of tea and biscuits and fruit at the League of Friends cafe, just to keep us going.

The Physiotherapist showed up around noon. Considering Michael had been admitted at 5.30 a.m. and that none of us had had any sleep, we thought this was disgraceful. I know this wasn't the girl's fault, there was evidently a lack of resources, but that didn't help our anxiety. The young physiotherapist agreed that what we'd been doing so far was correct but that it might have worked better had Michael been in a tipped up position on the bed. As he would not be put on the bed there was another technique we could try and that was to gently but firmly thump the front of his chest intermittently with the hand slightly cupped. When she demonstrated this it caused Michael to bring some frothy stuff up into his mouth, but it wasn't much.

The young lady suggested I persevere with this and she would review the situation later when the consultant had seen him. I was a little surprised that now Michael was an in-patient we still had to treat him ourselves. In my tiredness I resented this and felt very dissatisfied with his treatment My only comfort was that Michael might have preferred it this way.

Jim returned and I showed him how to do the new chesting technique. I was then able to go home for my refresher break.

During all this time Jim and I hadn't let either of our families know what was happening They had no idea what Michael was going through and didn't even know that he was in hospital We felt it best not to worry them at this stage.

Soon after I returned to the ward in the late afternoon the Consultant came round. That was traumatic in itself. Michael made noisy protests about being put on the bed for examination and afterwards, when putting him back in his chair, Jim was quite sharp with him.

The Consultant said that he obviously had a chest infection with some possible pneumonia developing. He would arrange for a chest x-ray and as soon as they could get a specimen of sputum off Michael they would get it analysed urgently and start treatment. In the meantime all we could do was continue as we were. He would review the situation the next day.

During the next hour or two we tried in vain to get a sputum specimen and Michael was becoming very tired and distressed.

"What's to become of me?" he asked.

"If they don't do any more than at present," I said, "we'll take you home and get Bobbie Mansell to give you a proper chest thumping. I'm sure she'll get a result."

He was so tired and to take his mind off his anxiety I suggested that we should take him to the bathroom, put him on the commode, freshen him up and then, if he still felt that he couldn't go to bed to sleep, get him comfortable enough to sleep in his wheelchair.

To our surprise he had no bowel trouble, was soon finished in the bathroom and felt a little better. I felt very distressed, though, when he still refused to go to bed. I stayed in the bathroom while Jim wheeled him back onto the ward. The sister happened to see him and she came over to me.

In tears now, I told her "He's so tired sister, and still too frightened to go to bed. How much longer can he go on like this?"

She was very kind and practical. She said she would help us to make him comfortable, padding him all round and piling his table in front of him with pillows, enough to allow him to rest his head.

"He'll probably fall asleep quite quickly, once comfortable, because he is exhausted" she said.

So this was what we did. When he was thus padded sister asked him

"Would you like some oxygen, Michael?"

"Yes please," he said, realising he needed it.

She connected him up to a portable oxygen cylinder and then left us.

Jim said "We'll have to be going home soon, we haven't slept since Friday night", whereupon Michael begged us to stay.

"I'm not going anywhere," I said, holding Michael's hand, and in that instant I knew that Michael wouldn't last the night. He had gone very pale now and shut his eyes. He looked very comfortable and after five or ten minutes I felt he was asleep.

I was about to tell Jim to go home if he was tired, as there was no point in both of us losing another night's sleep, when the Duty Doctor approached on his way down the ward. He glanced towards Michael and came over. He looked rather anxiously at him and before I could say "At last he's asleep", he snapped

"How long has he been like this?"

"About ten minutes," I said, and before I could say another word,

"Get him onto the bed, quickly!" he commanded Jim, who in bewilderment obeyed him. As he did so the doctor pressed some numbers on his bleeper and suddenly staff came running from all directions. I realised what was happening as the Crash Team arrived and sister pulled us away to her office.

"Oh no," I said to Jim.

"He's in cardiac arrest."

Then to sister "Tell them to mind his legs, please," I begged.

But I knew from my days in the Spinal Injuries Unit that attempting resuscitation was often a futile exercise. I had been on the wards on many occasions when Crash Teams had arrived and personally had never seen a survivor.

"It's no good" I told Jim.

"He won't come out of this, he's gone".

We held each other and wept. Then sister came to tell us what we knew already.

When the Crash Team had gone the young doctor came to talk to us. He was quite emotionally overcome himself, because of Michael's young age, I suppose.

"I'm so sorry" he said.

The Nursing Officer then came over to us. She was very emotional too and said they had now made Michael look nice for us. He looked very peaceful now, so we could see him and say our goodbyes properly.

"Goodbye my boy" I said and kissed him on his forehead.

"Goodbye son" Jim whispered behind me. Then we walked away.

The nursing officer asked if she could telephone someone to fetch us home but Jim declined. He wanted to drive himself. We thanked the staff and walked to the car park in a daze.

We were quite calm now, realising that Michael's heart had been weak to begin with so there was no chance he could have been resuscitated. I had often thought that if he was to die it should be peacefully in his sleep. That was more or less what had happened. He had been afraid for several hours of what was happening with his chest infection, but as soon as he'd been given the oxygen, I believe he knew no more after that.

The next thing we had to think about was telling our parents, which was going to be pretty harrowing because they didn't even know that Michael had been admitted to hospital.

When we walked into Fan and Mick's house at 9.30 that evening they were surprised to see us and their first words were "Where's Jack? You haven't left him on his own, have you?"

I started to tell them that he had been admitted to hospital in the early hours of Sunday morning, then I told them to sit down and blurted out "He's dead".

Their reaction was naturally one of shock and disbelief. Fan disappeared into the hall shouting,

"No! No! No! I don't believe you. You musn't say that, it's wrong."

"Not Jack, not my boy." Her voice trailed off as she sat down heavily on the stairs, defeated, realising the truth.

Jim went after her, brought her back in and made her sit down. The tears were running down Mick's face.

"Poor Jack" he muttered. "Poor Jack".

When Fan had calmed down Mick made us all a cup of tea and we talked. We told him and Fan all that had happened since we saw them the previous day. They said "You must go home now and get some rest."

I was worried about letting my mum and Harry know but they were not on the telephone. We thought it best to leave that till morning when perhaps Jim's brother or my friend Marion would fetch them to our house. I don't remember much of the rest of the evening except for a very strange thing that happened when Jim and I, as if expecting to see him there, walked into Michael's bedroom. There was a funny noise in there, a high-pitched continuous noise like the signal tone when a telephone number is unobtainable. We couldn't think what it was but eventually discovered that it was Michael's bedside clock. The battery was spent. It was uncanny. Time had indeed run out.

Next day we had so many callers, my friend Marion being the first. She immediately telephoned our GP's surgery. I was surprised when, within less than an hour, Dr Hughes called. He was very kind and comforting and asked if we'd like something to help us to sleep. Jim said he'd be all right but thought I should have something so Dr Hughes left me half a dozen little blue pills.

When he had gone Marion asked, "Have you two eaten?"

We hadn't thought about food. We were numb. She took charge, found some bacon and eggs, cooked them, and once it was in front of us we ate, realising that we were indeed hungry. Then she cleared up and went to see the Registrar for us. When she came back she brought my parents with her. Like Fan and Mick they were devastated.

We don't remember much of what happened in the next few days except that we automatically did all that had to be done, but we do remember everyone's kindness. Many friends called: colleagues from the hospital, Rita, Barry Francis Jones, Wagih El Masri, Gwilym Jones, and many others. Michael's friends called. That was one of the most emotional moments, all of us clinging together in our grief.

Prof telephoned our home, having been informed by Marion that Michael had passed away. His words were a great comfort and he invited Jim and I to go along and see him at his clinic the following week, which we did. We wanted to thank him for all his encouragement and help over the years and for being a true friend to Michael.

Carolyn Evans the Muscular Dystrophy Group Family Care Officer at the hospital came to see us. She was very kind and said all the right things. Then she said

"I'm going to ask rather a lot of you now, but I think you'll like what I'm going to suggest". She then went on to explain that nationally that particular week was 'Muscular Dystrophy Week' and she wondered if Jim and I would agree to loan all Michael's art work to exhibit at the hospital that coming Friday. This would be a kind of Memorial Exhibition that the general public could visit and appreciate Michael's talent and at the same time be made aware of Muscular Dystrophy, the difficulties of those who had the disease and the need to fight it with continuing research. They would be invited, but not pressured, to make donations to the Muscular Dystrophy Group.

Of course we agreed and I found it a great comfort, only five days after Michael's death, to sit in on the exhibition and answer any questions the visitors might ask. I felt so proud of Michael as people commented on his work.

Michael's old teacher, Gwyn Jones, contacted us a little later and organised an exhibition of Michael's work at Llangollen Library, which we felt was a great honour. The local press covered that.

Michael's funeral was very well attended and the vicar, Mr Villiers, spoke very movingly about his short, difficult but happy life. He also spoke about his artistic and design talents. Muckspreader, Trina, Swannick, Dawn and Michael's other young friends wept openly in the church.

Now that our wounded hearts are healing and we can look back without anger at the short time God had given Michael, we often think of our son as being in that 'big Design Centre' or 'big Art Gallery in the sky'. On those days when the sky looks particularly beautiful, or when there is a magnificent sunset, we say, "Michael's got his paintbrush out again".

Muckspreader told us that he always thinks of Michael on such days too and I believe, through knowing Michael, his young friends have more of an appreciation of art and beauty and human qualities than they would otherwise have done. He enriched their lives as they enriched his. They still cherish photographs of them all together, happy and laughing. They will never forget him nor will we. When Russell and Dawn were married and again when Muckspreader and Trina tied the knot soon afterwards, at both weddings there were tears in our eyes when Michael was remembered and mentioned in the speeches.

Muckspreader and Trina now have a beautiful baby boy called James. Russell and Dawn are also proud parents of a beautiful baby boy called Thomas. I hope that one day James and Thomas will know about Michael and his very special friendship with their parents.

Postscript

This story would not be complete without relating the dramatic family surprise that happened four years after Michael's passing.

My mother, God bless her, always wanting to do her share to help in some way when I was working and looking after Michael, would come to our house every Friday afternoon to clean and tidy the house for me. Following his death she wanted to continue doing this for she looked forward to seeing us and to the change of scene every week.

On Friday 18 September 1992 (a date I will never forget) I collected her as usual and took her to our house during my lunch break. She was very quiet during the journey and once we got into the house she asked me to sit down because she had something very important to tell me. I cannot remember her exact words as my mind was in a whirl when she told me I had a long lost half sister who had been adopted at birth and who suddenly, after 42 years, had traced her real mother.

Her adoptive parents named my sister (for that is how I think of her) Vanessa and she had been born when I was six years old. In her own mind mum had named her Rose Marie and had been devastated to part with her but it had been necessary because Vanessa's father - a local man - had left the scene and gone away. Mum was unmarried when I was born and no way could my grandparents afford to keep another child or put up with the stigma of illegitimacy again. My grandmother would have dearly loved to keep her but grandfather put his foot down. Mother was sent away to stay with a relative until it was all over. Mum had tried not to think about her child for all those years and for the rest of the family it was a closed book.

I was elated to know that I had a sister and I just hugged mum and we both cried. Mum was so glad that I felt that way. She had been in a huge dilemma for weeks, having been told by my Aunt Stella, who had been Vanessa's first contact, that her long lost daughter wished to meet her. My stepfather had no knowledge of that episode in my mother's life and she had been forced, now, to tell him. At the age of seventy, she was finally able to open the door in her mind to release the pain that she must have felt all those years ago when she had to give her daughter up. I could see the relief in her face at my reaction to the news and she told me how well Harry had taken it and how happy she was now that she felt able to meet Vanessa.

Auntie Stella had met Vanessa and her husband already and mum had been given a photograph of her, which she showed me. This time I was shocked and saddened to see in the photograph two boys, both in wheelchairs! Muscular Dystrophy had struck there too. I broke down at this juncture, clinging to mum and sobbing, thinking, "My sister has suffered double the heartache". Mum told me gently that the eldest of Vanessa's two boys, Scott, had died in May 1991, aged fifteen years.

I immediately knew I wanted to meet Vanessa and her family. Mum had been given a telephone number which I took from her, picked up the 'phone and dialled. There was no time like the present!

I broke the ice first "Hello 'sis'?"
"Its Gloria!" she shouted excitedly to her husband Tony in the background.
Then, "This is the best birthday present I've ever had!"
"No it isn't, the best is yet to come" I said.

"Here's the voice you've been longing to hear" and I gave mum the phone. What an emotional moment that was. I cannot begin to imagine how either of them felt. It was sheer coincidence that today was Vanessa's birthday. It's one she will never forget!

We arranged to travel that Sunday to West Kirby, where Vanessa lived, to meet her and her family. She explained that she had not yet told her adoptive parents about her search for mum and its conclusion so would appreciate meeting away from the house initially.

Jim drove us to West Kirby, where we met Vanessa in the town centre. There was no mistaking her - she was so like mum. After all the emotional greetings, hugs and kisses she got into the car and Jim drove us to the Marina where we talked and talked. Then she decided we should go to the house so that we could meet Tony, Matthew, daughter Wendy and grandson Sean. Vanessa had warned us not to mention Michael in front of Matthew because he had not got over the death of his brother Scott.

We had to steel ourselves to meet Matthew, hiding our emotions considerably, but it was not as hard as I thought it would be. He was a bit reserved and quiet, probably bewildered by all this excitement. He was severely affected by the disease. There was a little resemblance to Michael and with the same handicap his posture in the wheelchair was very similar. We grew to love him very much. Matthew died in September 1998 and had never been told the truth about Michael. He knew we had a son who died but didn't know how or why. I expect he read between the lines but we didn't want to add to his fears about his own mortality by telling him.

Vanessa eventually told her adoptive parents, Beryl and Allen, about finding her real mother. They were a little hurt that she had felt unable to tell them what she was doing at the outset but other than that their attitude was of welcoming an enlargement of the family circle. Not a surprising attitude when you think they had fostered thirty-six children, adopted three and had two of their own over the years! Meeting them was a wonderful experience and we warmed to them instantly. Mum thanked them with all her heart for taking Vanessa and giving her their love and care over the years.

Vanessa, mum and I have seen a lot of each other since that reunion. Talking about our common bond, the loss of our respective sons, Vanessa and I like to think that Scott, Matthew and Michael, unknown to each other as cousins on earth, are now together in heaven.

The search for the relief and cure of Muscular Dystrophy goes on. The fight must go on and we must continue to support research into this crippling disease, not only to find a cure but to make the lives of those severely and irreversibly affected as happy, full and comfortable as possible.